GRAVEN IMAGES

GAIL TANZER

i

ISBN: 978-1-950613-16-8
Copyright 2019

This biography is a fictional dramatization based on real events and was drawn from a variety of sources, including published materials and interviews. For narrative purposes, the book contains fictionalized scenes, composite and representative characters and dialogue, and time compression. The views and opinions expressed in the story are those of the characters only and do not necessarily reflect or represent the views and opinions held by individuals on which those characters are based.

Taylor and Seale Publishing, LLC.
Daytona Beach Shores, Florida 32118
taylorandsealebooks.com
386-481-0502   386-760-8987

(Cover Design by Jill McClain)

Dedication

To Jean M. Pierre

With thanks for his extensive research assistance and for giving me invaluable feedback.

Part One

ONE

I didn't know what happened. All I knew was I felt like a rubber band that got stretched too far and snapped. I had snapped before, but each time it took me by surprise.

Knocking and yelling at my apartment door, my neighbor broke the spell.

"What are you doing in there, Gussie? What's wrong?" My chest heaved as I dropped my hammer and shuffled to the door.

When I let Cynthia in, her mouth fell open in shock. "What have you done? Are those your sculptures on the floor... broken into pieces?" I nodded with my head down like a misbehaving child being reprimanded. Cynthia took command. "Sit down with me, Gussie. This is not like you."

We made our way to my couch. Every breath was accompanied by a sob. Cynthia took my hand.

Her eyes and voice became gentle, sympathetic. "Why did you do this? You loved these sculptures like they were members of your family."

My sobbing turned to full-on weeping. Cynthia put her hand on my shoulder. "It's okay, it's okay, Baby."

Finally, I was able to eek out, "They...they seemed to be accusing me."

"Of what?"

"Of being a failure."

Always practical, Cynthia said, "You know statues can't talk, Gussie."

"I know, I know," I mumbled. "I said they 'seemed' to be accusing me."

1

"You're one of the most famous people in Harlem, and you just made that gigantic statue for the World's Fair. It was so popular! How could you think you're a failure?"

I looked away. "It's hard to explain, Cynthia, but I gotta figure this out."

"I can sit with you while you think," Cynthia crooked her head towards me like a mother talking lovingly to her child.

"I appreciate it, but I'm done. I did what I did, and now it's over. I'm glad you stopped me, but I'd like to be alone for a while."

My neighbor got up and inched her way to my apartment door looking back at me occasionally. "All right, Baby, but you call me or come over if you ever think you're losin' it again." I assured her I would.

If Cynthia could have seen me when I gave a speech at the Chicago Auditorium Theater just two weeks earlier, she would have thought I was the most composed person in the world. Not like this lunatic.

Eventually my breathing returned to normal. I got out a broom and swept the largest shards of clay into a dustpan. All my work, all those hours of creating — swept away in a matter of moments.

Although I didn't know what hit me, I did know why. Mrs. Johnson, the wife of one of my subjects, had asked the same haunting question my daughter, Irene, had asked just a week before: "What are you going to do now?" I had no idea.

Now that I felt saner perhaps I could figure out where to go from here, but I knew it would take some serious soul-searching. What happened on this day was not my first uncontrollable outburst, but I wanted it to be my last.

TWO

My hometown of Green Cove Springs, Florida is where everything started.

I was a slip of a girl, slender but strong. Both my parents were children as slaves before Abraham Lincoln set us free. Although my mama gave birth to fourteen children, only nine of us survived past the age of two. Mama and Daddy didn't have time to give us much attention, but my mama always reminded me of the circumstances of my birth.

From the time I was four, Mama told me on my leap year birthday, "Gussie, your birth was different than any of my other babies. You was born on February 29th, 1892, on the dark side of the moon, which means you'll be special someday and live to be 102."

The dark side of the moon? Live to be 102? Eek!

"Why do you say I was born on the dark side of the moon?"

"You was born when the moon wasn't shining anymore, and the sun hadn't come up yet."

Mama continued, "Another special thing about you, Gussie. You was born with a caul around your head."

I couldn't help but ask, "What was that, Mama?"

"It was a watery sack. Though it was watery, it was strong. The midwife had to cut it open to get you out."

"Yuck!" I groaned.

"That caul, and when you was born—they're both like omens that mean you'll make somethin' special of yourself someday."

My daddy snorted when he heard what Mama said, "You and your superstitions. There ain't nothin' about them in the Bible."

3

As soon as Daddy walked away, we went back to our conversation.

I asked, "What do you mean I'll be special?"

"It means you'll 'complish somethin' so important that the world takes notice of you."

The way my mama put her arm around my shoulder and looked down at me with such love and admiration made me feel doing something special could be sweet. I guess that's what started my going all out to succeed.

*****

I never made mud pies. My sisters and brothers acted as if that was all you could make from the layers of light blue, yellow, red and brown earth in a clay pit near our house. I wondered what my future would have been like if we hadn't found that clay.

As a little kid, I did my share of chores, but all I wanted was to get to the clay pit to form the chickens, ducks and barnyard animals I saw every day. The pit was next to Black Creek that trickled into the nearby St. John's River. On dry days, we kids used an old, leaky bucket to collect water from the creek so we could get the clay wet enough to mold.

Seeing as how the clay pit was a little way from our house and there were plenty of trees around, no one saw us kids high-tailin' it over there. We had to sneak, because Mama and Daddy didn't like us going to the pit. If Mama saw we had clay on our hands or clothes, she would scold us about getting dirty. Then Daddy would reprimand us for making "graven images." After giving us a Bible sermon on idol worship, Daddy would start in on alligators by the creek.

We snuck over there anyhow. We'd fight over who could use the bucket first. Within no time, though, my sisters and brothers would lose interest and leave. I could sit working there for hours, going back and forth with that bucket, massaging the clay into animals, humming church music, and swatting away mosquitoes.

Hating Mama's scolding and becoming increasingly bored with the clay pit, my siblings eventually gave up their clay work for other activities like playing catch-me-if-you-can and hide-and-seek behind the mossy, old oak trees. I joined in with them sometimes, but mostly I did my clay molding. I even stole a kitchen knife to add details to my barnyard animals. My mother could probably see bits of clay on me, but she pretended not to notice. Somehow she understood my need.

When I worked with the clay, I went into my own world. My little legs were so strong that it hardly bothered me to stay crouching down so I wouldn't get "dirty." One day I got so involved I forgot about the gators Daddy warned us about. As I scooped my bucket into the creek, a gator brushed against my hand. When I saw his knobby eyes staring up at me, I took off running as fast as I could. The gator moved just as quickly. I was scared half to death, but eventually that gator crunched down on my bucket and stopped to rip it apart, losing all interest in me. I breathed a sigh of relief. In my child's mind, I thought that if the gator only tore my arm or leg off, my daddy would have finished the job for not listening to him.

On another afternoon, I squatted by the pit putting finishing touches on my latest duck that I named Lucy. I admired the way I made her beak and how I made the feathers in her tail stand up just so. While the clay was still soft, I made a hollow opening so I could put my hand inside and move her beak.

I said, "Hi, Lucy. Hope you like the name I chose for you."

Like a ventriloquist, I had my duck answer back. "*Hi to you,*" she said. "*Thanks for making me. Can we be friends?*"

"Of course, Lucy, we can be best of friends. I'll tell you all my secrets."

But my conversation with Lucy didn't last long. Suddenly a dark shadow loomed over us. I stood up and turned. It was my daddy.

He roared, "Augusta Christine Fells, what did I tell you about coming down here?" When Daddy called me Augusta instead of Gussie, I knew I was in trouble.

"You know you shouldn't be goin' to the pit." Daddy's eyes popped with a fury that said, *How dare you disobey your father?*

"What you hidin' behind you?" Daddy stormed. He put his big hand behind my back and tore Lucy from my grasp.

Looking down at little Lucy, he squeezed her so tight that her perfect beak and tail got all mushed up. "These animals! They the work of the devil! You're making idols, graven images that the Bible warns against."

Daddy pulled back his arm and, with all his might, threw Lucy into the creek. Since the creek was lined with trees, vines and undergrowth, I couldn't see where Lucy landed, but when I heard the plop, I had to fight back tears. Daddy ordered me to go home. I ran.

Crying and running, I lamented, *I hate my father. I hate my father.* Although I had just made Lucy, I felt she was my friend, and now my daddy made her drown. Losing Lucy was painful, but by the time I got home, I realized there were more ducks from where she came. I would make a new Lucy, whether Daddy liked it or not. I'd just make sure he didn't see.

*****

My mama and daddy stayed busy from sunrise to sunset, working in town and tending the piece of land that was all their own. Once when I was helping my father work the soil in our vegetable garden, I asked him how he got our little farm. "I got this land from a White man named Mr. Clinch for a small price. It's land nobody else wanted. There's not enough people in Florida, because it's too hot and full of mosquitoes down here. My sister back in Mississippi said she wouldn't live in Florida if they paid her. She's afraid alligators would be as plentiful as mosquitoes."

I asked, "If it was so bad, why did you buy it?"

Daddy said, "I wanted to break out and be my own man, my own boss. Land, I thought, was the answer."

"Are you sorry you bought it?"

Turning over a big shovelful of dirt, Daddy answered, "No. I love this land. Course, it's not enough to support us. Your mama and me have to work extra jobs. Thank the Good Lord that Green Cove Springs has plenty of work with the tourists and all. But we live off the food from this land, and it's mine."

My hometown was a big deal back in the 1890s, because it had a hot spring that bubbled up out of the earth. Visitors came from miles away to bathe in a pool that captured most of its water. The rest flowed into a narrow stream that went about thirty feet down to the St. John River. I couldn't understand why the white people liked the water. It smelled like rotten eggs! Daddy said the smell came from sulfur. According to Daddy, the guests ignored the bad smell, because they thought the spring water had healing powers.

My parents heard the guests talking about having rheumatism or arthritis or lumbago. I had no idea what those things were, but judging from how the visitors looked, they all had to do with old age. Among our town's twenty hotels, one had a cemetery for those who "didn't make it."

There were a lot of jobs for Coloreds at the hotels, but, of course, we knew our place. Especially when it came to the water. Nobody had to tell us we shouldn't go in. If we did, we knew the Whites would think we'd tainted it.

Some visitors got to Green Cove Springs from the north by railroad. Others took steamboats from nearby Jacksonville down the St. John River. My mama was a laundress at The Magnolia Hotel, one of the largest hotels in town. Near the springs, it had a sign in front that said it had 200 rooms.

Mama was short, slim and strong from all her hard work. Her skin looked like soft, buttery caramel. Most days she wore a simple cotton dress—like the one I wore—that helped her stay as cool as possible. The only time she fixed her hair and wore a fancy outfit with a hat was when we went to church. I'd fight to get a seat next to her, and then I'd stare at her like she was one of the rich tourists.

She looked so pretty: her eyes, nose and ears were all so fine and delicate. When I got cleaned up for church, people sometimes said I looked just like my mama. Before I was grown, the attention made me grab my mama's dress and hide my face in it. But when I got older—like 14 or so—I would acknowledge the comment with a proud smile.

I felt Mama was beautiful even though her eyes always looked tired. Cooking and cleaning for us and working with all those strong washing soaps didn't help. My mama was a quiet woman. I got the feeling that she worked so hard that she didn't want to waste any extra energy by talking unless she had to.

Unlike my mama, my daddy loved to talk. He had a dark, chocolaty skin that looked different in different lights. During the workweek, he wore overalls and a white muslin shirt. Tall, broad-chested, and full of muscles, he looked like he could move a mountain. However, for church on Sundays he took on a whole other appearance. He'd trim his mustache and short beard and put on his one suit with a vest and white shirt.

When Daddy wanted us to appreciate what little we had, he'd say, "You kids don't know how good you got it. My papa got sold to a different master when I was little. We missed him so much, but after we were freed, Papa found his way back to us. This here family won't ever be split apart!"

Daddy worked at the brick company where a new clay pit was built, and he painted walls at the hotels, but his real passion was preaching. He would substitute-preach at different churches in our county. The man could spout a Bible passage for anything. Being raised as a slave, he didn't know how to read or write at first, but it was tradition that other preachers helped new ones read and repeat scriptures. So, Daddy learned how to read.

I wished I didn't have a preacher for a daddy. He found a Bible passage to forbid any type of pleasure us kids might have. When he lectured too much, Mama hit Daddy's knee and warned him quietly, "You stop it, now." She was the only person he'd listen to.

I always knew I was different from my brothers and sisters. I thought back to how I acted when a typical Florida hurricane hit. We lived in a one story wooden house. Years later, after moving to New York City, I thought of it more as a shack. Back then we didn't mind. It was home, and all us Colored people lived like that in Green Cove Springs.

Seeing as how Florida was almost always hot, we stayed outside a lot anyhow. Walls divided the house into three bedrooms and an area for cooking with a big table where we sat and ate, but never together because the table didn't have room for everyone. For sleeping, there were four large mattresses in two of the bedrooms, and my parents slept on one in the third room. Several of us had to sleep together. Mama made the mattresses by sewing together big pieces of cloth and stuffing them with cotton. There was no shortage of cotton in the nearby fields.

When this particular hurricane came our way, the other kids huddled together on the mattresses with quilts over them. There was a lot of howling and creaking from the heavy winds and blowing trees. That afternoon I had "borrowed" a slate from school, and during the storm I sat in a corner by myself, sketching new poses for my clay animals.

My mama crouched by me. "Gussie, why don't you go sit under the quilts with the other children? It'd be a comfort to you."

I hated to put down my slate, but, dutifully, I got up and joined the closest group. My brothers and sisters alternated between giggling and screaming, and I gradually joined in. However. I was just as happy being alone.

THREE

We had to walk two miles to get to our one room schoolhouse. But that was all right...at first.

The problem was that the clay kept calling me. *Come make something out of me today. Don't you love how I bend to your every whim? Don't you like the cute little animals you can mold and talk to?'*

I tried to resist the call, but I couldn't. I skipped school sometimes. With all the kids in our house getting ready at once, I thought my parents would never notice. After I made my animal friends, I put them in the bushes by the creek so they would dry and, most importantly, be out of sight of my daddy.

One day when I skipped school and began molding at the pit I saw that shadow and heard that booming voice again, "Get away from there right now, and go get me a switch! I'll teach you to do what I say!"

I felt my shoulders sag. When I got a switch and gave it to Daddy, he took it to my legs. After he switched me, he said, "Go on home now, and don't come back here no more."

I didn't listen. Three or four times a week Daddy licked me for going to the clay pit. Later on when I gave interviews I told people that he almost whipped all the art out of me.

On one of the times my father found me working with the clay, he repeated his familiar lecture, "I done told you, Gussie, this is blasphemy. The way you love these little statues and talk to them makes me think of worshippin' idols. You know God forbids idolatry. You should busy yourself with readin' the Bible."

With my arms down at my sides and my hands clenched into fists, I got the courage to talk back for once. I looked up into his eyes and, loud and clear, said, "I don't even know how to read yet!"

"Do what I tell you, and don't disobey me, Augusta Christine Fells! I don't want God to have to punish you." This time my father carried his own switch. As he pulled it back, maybe God or my guardian angel intervened. He simply said, "I'm serious about this, Gussie," and walked away like he knew he couldn't win and didn't want to keep hurting me.

I knew my daddy was serious. But I was serious too. I loved the feeling of clay in my hands and the chance to make it into something special. The older I got the more details I etched into the clay with twigs and my stolen knife. Sometimes I created the horses, pigs, and cow we had on our farm, but mostly I liked making ducks and chickens. Ducks swam in the creek by the clay pit, and I would stare and stare at them so I could copy each of their features. I was proud of my creations, and I enjoyed talking with them like I did with Lucy.

Although I preferred molding the earth, I did attend school most days. There were 48 children in our one room schoolhouse. Exuberant were we when we tumbled through the door of that big old, wood framed building. We'd be laughing and out of order until our teacher Mr. Johnson told us to sit down and be quiet. All it took to keep us in line was Mr. Johnson paddling a kid once in front of the whole class. If someone did something mean to someone else, Mr. Johnson pointed to a framed, embroidered sign on the wall that said, "Do unto others as you would have them do unto you."

Mr. Johnson knew how to make us behave, but he was basically a sweet man who loved learning. He told us he had attended Florida A&M College in Tallahassee, that he enjoyed going to school and hoped we'd keep up our education. As soon as the bell rang for recess, Mr. Johnson would pull out a book of his own and start reading. I hoped that Mr. Johnson realized how well he taught us. Like most of my classmates, I mastered the essentials of reading, writing and arithmetic.

Just about every time we had a spelling bee, I won. I always studied my spelling words really hard. Whenever I won a bee I got that feeling of doing something special. I loved feeling important, like I'd accomplished something. But I also saw one of its costs—the scowls of my fellow students whom I'd defeated.

When I got home from school on those days, I would find a quiet time to be with my mama—peeling potatoes or hanging clothes on the line—and I'd whisper to her so my sisters and brothers wouldn't hear, "I won the spelling bee today, Mama." She'd hug me and whisper back, "See, I told you you'd be a success."

FOUR

I had a job on the farm. Every morning when our rooster crowed I had to go outside and feed the chickens and gather their new eggs. Sometimes it was hard for me to get out of bed so early, but I liked greeting the chickens and hearing them cluck back to me in chicken language.

I wanted to name our animals. However, early on, I learned not to get too attached. Witnessing Daddy wring the neck of the chicken I called Annabelle was enough to stop me. My father noticed me crying. In a soft voice, he said, "Gussie, we need these animals for food. If we can't eat 'em, we'll starve." I looked at Daddy closer than I ever had before. This was the first time I realized he really cared about me.

*****

Whites never came to bother us in our part of town, and we didn't bother them. The one time I remember an uproar over how Whites acted was when my father came home from his bricklaying job and pounded his fist on the table. "Can you believe those White people? The guys at the pit say that up Orange Park where I just preached last week they arrested a White teacher for teaching Whites and Coloreds in the same room."

Stirring greens on our wood-burning stove, Mama said, "What kinda foolishness is that?"

"It's ridiculous foolishness is what it is," Daddy fumed. "That school is run by church people and their missionaries. I think they put the teacher in jail—the poor fellow." He pulled at his little beard. "I thought they freed us over thirty years ago."

"It's a shame. What sorta school is it? " Mama asked.

"The guys at the brickyard said it taught the children how to sew, be carpenters, put on roofs. The

14

school was real nice to them. They gave 'em good meals and let 'em stay in their big house if they wanted…"

Mama interrupted. "What made them think they could arrest that teacher, though?"

"Some new law just got passed in Florida about Whites and Coloreds not being allowed in the same classroom."

Mama was getting as hot as the greens she was cooking. She turned with her mixing fork to Daddy and raised her voice. "The nerve! I remember when we were first freed we were so happy. We didn't know exactly where to go, what to do, but it seemed like things would finally go our way. Remember how they even let Colored men run for office?"

Daddy said, "That sure didn't last. I think that's because after the war they had those soldiers around making sure everyone behaved. But, in no time, the soldiers were gone, and now the Whites done passed all kinds of laws to keep us in our place."

Mama sighed. "Now I think I remember someone talkin' about them. Jim Crow laws, that's what they call 'em. Separate but equal."

"Yep, now they'll be makin' Colored bathrooms, train cars, and schools," Daddy fumed.

Speaking louder than I'd ever heard her, my mama said, "Yeah, and I bet our facilities will never get cleaned. Call that equal!"

I let all of this talk go in one ear and out the other. Like most kids I lived in the here and now, and if something didn't affect me directly, the words rolled off me like a quilt pulled away by my sister in the middle of the night. I just kept sleeping unless I got really cold. Likewise, I didn't worry about the Jim Crow laws until they affected me.

The place where we derived the most comfort was church. Twice a week we went. I loved being in the choir. Although most of the grownups were slaves as children and hadn't been taught how to read or write, they remembered every word of the songs. I sang the words mechanically without paying much attention to their meaning. They were full of suffering, emphasizing how we were all in it together: poor, Colored, and doing the best we could in our own little world. I just sang the words from memory, not realizing how true I would find them to be.

By the time I was fifteen, I still made animals at the clay pit. My daddy continued to warn me against it, but said I was too old to take the switch to. At my age, Mother Nature got involved. Something else—besides sculpting—sparked my interest.

FIVE

My attention went to a young man—maybe about twenty—who lived in a little house down the road. Slender and the height of most young men, he usually wore dungarees and a white t-shirt...a tight one at that. His small but noticeable muscles bulged out of the sleeves. The way he kept his face clear of a moustache or beard made his handsome features stand out. Always smiling, he seemed to see life in the sunniest of colors. My father talked with him outside sometimes, and I gathered his name was John.

One morning when he was saddling up his horse, looking like he was heading off for work, I decided to strike up a conversation. "Hi, that's a pretty big horse there."

"Yeah, she is. I call her Sandy, since she's colored like sand."

I felt shy, but I really wanted to make this fellow's acquaintance. "My name is Augusta, but everyone calls me 'Gussie.'"

"Well, then, is it okay if I call you 'Gussie'?"

"Go right ahead."

"My name is John. Pleased to meet you." He extended his hand towards me.

I put my hand out in return, and we shook.

"Gotta go!" I yelled as I ran off to make it to school on time.

I found myself making excuses to pass by John's house. Often he sat on his front steps whittling. I complimented him on his carvings, and it seemed we were becoming friends. Within a couple of months, that changed. It started when John asked me to come inside so he could show me his house. I was surprised at how plain it was. The windows even had potato sacks on a rod he pulled open during the day and closed at night.

"This place needs a woman's touch," John said as he came near to where I stood and looked into my eyes.

I met his gaze, and he gave me a tiny kiss on the lips.

I couldn't believe I was being kissed. However, I was too shy to let myself enjoy it. I pulled away and said, "Gotta go. Think my mama needs me now."

"I understand," he said with a smile, like he knew I was fibbing.

When I went to bed that night, I thought about that kiss. It was short, but John's lips were soft and sweet. I wished I let myself taste them longer.

A tumble of thoughts played with my sleepy mind. I knew I was getting ahead of myself, but I thought, *John could be my boyfriend. Why not? Maybe we could even get married someday, but that would be way off.* I was only 15, but my older sister got married at 16. In Florida, there were no laws against it.

I tried to imagine what my parents would say, if we ever wanted to get married. They weren't happy about my sister jumping the broom so young, but they didn't stand in her way either. Now my sister followed in our mother's footsteps, being a laundress at a hotel. Her husband was a blacksmith. They already had two children.

I decided I liked John and would wait to see what might happen between us. It was really early to be thinking about this stuff. Maybe marriage would come, but I definitely didn't feel ready to be a mother. I still loved working with clay and going to school. Having a child would leave no time for those pleasures. And what about doing something special with my life like Mama predicted?

John and I continued seeing each other. He often took me riding on his big horse. There was an open field nearby, and I loved the sensation of speed and of having my arms around his waist.

I found out that John's last name was Moore. He liked school just like me, but he had to quit after sixth grade to help his parents on their farm. Eventually, he left his family in Middleburg—a one day horse and wagon ride from Green Cove Springs—to make more money for himself and build a better life than his parents'. He said he was well on his way by laying bricks like my daddy and bartending at one of the fancy hotels in town.

We spent a lot of time together. One thing led to another, and soon kissing was not enough. One afternoon I found myself lying in his bed with him and wanting to get to know every part of his body, but I felt it was wrong. I pulled away from John and said, "We shouldn't do this."

He kept his hand on my arm and asked ever so sweetly, "Why don't we get married?"

I gulped.

John continued, "I need a good woman to fix up this place and lay with me at night. It's lonely in this house." And then he added in a quiet, stumbling way like he couldn't quite get the out the words, "Besides, I feel happy when I'm with you. And I gotta tell you, Gussie, you're the best-lookin' girl I ever saw."

I felt like that four year-old girl who got shy when complimented on my looks, but I treasured John's praise. Yet I had to bring out some important points. "I would have to help my mother and to work with clay and to go to school."

"I would want you to stay in school and help your mama. But maybe your parents wouldn't mind having one less mouth to feed."

I frowned. Although I was far from being spoiled, I hoped my parents wouldn't want to get rid of me.

John looked like he regretted his last comment. "They probably still want you with them, but maybe I can talk with your father."

"Just wait. Let's take things a little slower," I said in a grownup way.

Unfortunately, I couldn't go slower with John. I just loved him too much. Yet I didn't want to commit that terrible sin of "fornication," as Daddy called it. So, getting married would give me permission to love John in a physical way without going to hell.

A few weeks later something happened that really pushed me into John's arms. It had to do with the babies. Since three of my siblings had already died before they were two, I tried not to get close to the babies. However, my newest baby sister seemed to take a special liking to me. Starting from the age of three months, she looked me right in the eyes and smiled when I dressed her. If she cried and no one could comfort her, Mama said, "You try her, Gussie." I would put her in my arms and walk her back and forth and, in no time, she would fall asleep on my shoulder. I couldn't help but love her. She loved me so much.

Until she was about eight months old, she was healthy as could be. She was chubby too which was a good sign, but one day when she was crawling she just plopped on the floor and stayed like that. I picked her up, and she went limp in my arms.

"Aw, you must be tired," I said and put her to bed. Fifteen minutes later she started screaming. When Mama and I went to look at her, we saw her scrunching her arms and legs together like she was having cramps. She threw up. I picked her up. Before I could clean her, she got sick again.

Mama cried, "Oh, no, not another baby…"

I looked at Mama and commanded her, "Don't say that!"

My mother sent my older brother to the other side of town where a woman lived who knew ways of healing people.

It seemed to take forever, but finally she came. In the meantime, my baby sister showed no signs of improving. When the healer saw what was happening, she said, "I've seen this before."

The woman had a bag tied around her waist, and from it she took spearmint leaves. She asked for a knife and a board, cut the leaves into tiny pieces, and requested some water. After she mixed the spearmint with the water, she forced the drink into my sister's mouth. My poor baby sister let out a blood-curdling scream.

The healer said, "I got some down her, though. You must get her to swallow this again later on. In a few hours, I'll come back with leeches. We'll be needin' to get the bad blood out."

My mother and I shrieked. Mama cried, "This is what happened to two of my other babies! The same thing."

The healer said, "Maybe we caught it in time. I'll be back soon."

My sister's situation went from bad to worse. Her chills turned into a burning fever. My father prayed over her. I squeezed her hand and kissed her forehead. Then I had to leave.

I ran to John's. It was a Saturday afternoon, and he was home. Seeing my state, he wrapped his arms around me and had me sit on his bed where he held me for a long time.

Before the healer returned with the leeches, Mama came over to John's. It was written all over Mama's face. My sister didn't make it. Mama put her arms around me and cried. We held onto each other— hopelessly— like we were going down in a sinking ship. No words could console.

*****

Now living at my house was sorrowful. I wouldn't go to the baby's funeral. I just wanted to remember the good times when my sister smiled at me and laid her head on my shoulder.

I started spending more time at John's. One day I talked with Mama who was moping around as much as me.

"Mama, you know how much time I spend with John."

"I know. He seems like a nice young man."

"He's been asking me to marry him," I said in a quiet voice, not knowing how she'd feel.

"You're so young, Gussie."

I went on to tell her how kind John was and how he wanted me to stay in school even if we were married. I assured her that since I'd live just down the road I'd come over and help with the cooking or whatever else she needed.

Looking disappointed but not forlorn, she said, "Well, I guess your older sister could keep helping me too. And John does seem like he'd take good care of you. That's the most important thing." I appreciated Mama's understanding.

And, so, Mama talked Daddy into the marriage. He did a quick ceremony with only a few of us at our little church, and John and I became Mr. and Mrs. Moore.

True to his word, John never kept me from going to school or shaping my clay figures. He didn't mind if I scurried over to help my parents. My father and John kept up their friendship, and all was going well. That was until something happened.

All along, John said he had a special way of us being together that would keep me from getting pregnant. It didn't work. For the first time, I yelled at John. "Why did you make me believe you knew how to keep me from getting pregnant?"

"That's what my daddy told me to do. I'm so sorry, Gussie. I didn't mean for this to happen." He said this with such pain in his voice that I knew he was sincere. "But the other part is I love you, and having a baby together...Well, it could be a happy thing." John smiled at me sheepishly. I frowned.

"I don't know about that. It's harder for a mother," I lamented.

The thought of having a baby when I was so young —only 16—kept me awake at night. During the pregnancy, I worried. How could I love another little one who could be taken away in the blink of an eye? How would I be able to continue my schooling and do my clay molding?

Growing bigger by the month, I kept going to school until I could hardly walk. I knew what it was like when the baby was ready to come. I had seen it enough with my mother. When it was my time, I had John rush over to my parents' and then over to the house of Mother Jones, who delivered nearly everyone's babies.

I never felt so much pain in my life, but, thankfully, it only lasted a few hours. After Mother Jones cleaned her up, she placed our new baby girl on my chest. I was filled with tenderness for this child who we named Irene.

Having a baby was very commonplace. After the birth, my mother stayed for maybe an hour and then went on her way. I don't think my father looked in. Even though I had plenty of experience raising my younger brothers and sisters, taking care of my own baby struck terror in me. I didn't say anything, but John could see something was wrong. I hardly had energy to dress and didn't fix any food for us. One day John walked out the door, saying, "Be right back, Gussie." He returned with my mother.

Mama's eyes were sympathetic. "Is this hard for you, Gussie?"

Sniffing back tears, I acknowledged, "Yes, Mama, very hard."

My mama seemed to understand. Perhaps she felt like this herself—at least with her first baby. She started coming over for a couple hours at a time. She cooked and cleaned and held little Irene.

After a week or so, Mama said in a tender voice, "Think you ready to manage her by yourself?"

"I don't know, but I'll try," I said.

Now I was on my own with Irene when John was at work. Thankfully, it was summer so I didn't miss any school. However, fear clutched my heart every time I bathed, fed or changed my daughter. That's because I dreamed at night that she would be lying on the bed next to me and I would shove her off onto the floor. In the dream, I couldn't tell if I did this on purpose or by mistake. Guilt gnawed at me that such a horrible vision ran through my mind. I couldn't tell anyone. I had a hard time sleeping for fear the dream would return or I would actually do something so terrible.

My eyes were baggy, and I didn't eat much. John and my mother could see that something was still wrong. They gave the baby and me big smiles. The baby responded, but I could only come up with fake smiles.

I was so glad to go back to school in the fall. My older sister, who was a homebody, took care of Irene when I was gone. My mother enjoyed being around Irene too even though she had plenty to do with her laundry job and cooking and cleaning for the other kids still at home. She said there was something special about being a grandma. Mama loved it when Irene got chubby cheeks and rolls of fat on her arms and legs. I finally quit having the scary dream, but, remembering how my baby brothers and sisters died, I was afraid that something bad could still happen.

Of course, I felt overworked. I cooked, cleaned, took care of my baby (when she wasn't at Grandma's), and did my homework.

When Irene turned two, my mother said, "If my baby was gonna die, it was before she turned two. Irene will live!"

I was happy about that, but the truth was I had tried too hard to not become attached to her. Irene loved to go to my mother's. And, honestly, I didn't mind.

But having a baby at my young age did not keep me from making things out of clay. I'd run down to the clay pit, put as much clay as I could into a wooden bucket, and carry it home. I tried doing something altogether new and different—making a sculpture of a person's head, namely my husband's. It was small, just the size of a man's clenched fist. John was patient enough to sit for me. This was so different from molding the ducks and barnyard animals, since they were never at rest.

With John, I could look at him straight in the eye for long periods. He didn't have a problem with this, and neither did I. While it was interesting to shape John's physical features—like his close-cropped hair, his nose, his forehead, his chin—it was most challenging to capture how his lips turned up in a slight smile, how he cocked his head to the side, and how his eyes were open wide with amazement. That was what made him John. When I showed him the finished piece, he grabbed me under my arms, lifted me up, and exclaimed, "You are the best, Gussie! It looks just like me!" The sweet sound of success!

On an unusually cool afternoon in February, John and I had an enjoyable time with our little daughter, who was now about two years old. I had her squat by a barrel filled with my wet clay. I said, "Irene, feel the clay." Then I took her little hands and had her touch it. She drew back at first, seeing as how she'd never felt such slippery stuff. But then I made a snake for her and showed how she could roll the clay back and forth between her hands. When she tried it, she squealed with delight.

After Irene tired of the clay, John picked her up by her hands and spun her around. Irene laughed and laughed. Eventually, John said, "The sun's going down. I might be late for work. I better get going."

He went in and put on his white shirt and bow tie, because he was working his bartending job. He came out of the house looking worried. "I still have to saddle Sandy. I hope I won't be late."

I said, "Now, don't worry so much. Like Mama says, 'Haste makes waste.'"

John gave me a quick peck on the cheek, saddled our horse and took off with her like a bolt of lightning.

I yelled, "Be careful, John!"

The sun was setting, bathing everything in shadows.

John didn't come home at his usual time. I prayed. "Dear Jesus, please bring my husband home safely." I paced the floors and then sat on our kitchen chair, hoping any minute I would see John walk through the back door. However, all was quiet. A quiet that was deafening.

The moment the sun began to rise I hurried over to my parents'. When my older sister answered the door, I immediately handed Irene to her. I roused my brother to fetch the buggy and go look with me for John.

A little voice told me, This could be embarrassing if John just stayed out all night drinking or, worse yet, was with another woman.

I had my brother trace John's usual path with me. When we got to the big, open field where John and I loved to ride, I saw them from a distance: two shadowy objects lying on the ground where the field ended and a tree-lined path began. I heard a horse whinnying in pain. When we got close enough, my worst fear came true. It was John and our horse. It looked like the horse had tripped on a big, downed tree limb. It kicked and screamed and frothed at the mouth.

I lay by John and caressed his cold, rigid body. My brother got his rifle out from the buggy. When he put the horse out of his misery, I felt like a bullet went through my heart. My pain was almost unbearable. My brother put John's body into the back of our buggy. We rode to the undertaker's. My pain only got worse as my brother laid John over his shoulders and brought him into the building. I remained in the buggy. The last thing I remember about my dear John were his legs flapping over my brother's back. My heart felt like it cracked in half.

Just like when my baby sister passed, I couldn't make myself attend John's funeral. My mother and father came to tell me how wonderful the ceremony was and how people lined the sides of the road as the undertaker's long buggy and a stream of loved ones walked behind to escort John to the cemetery.

Daddy crowed, "Our people may be poor, but we know how to honor our dead." I think I heard my mother kick him and say, "Hush."

Mama was right. I didn't want to hear about John being dead. I just wanted to stay as I was—motionless on our mattress, trying not to think about anything.

My mother brought food and drink to me, but I ignored it. Irene stayed with my parents and, because of her young age, she hardly knew what was going on.

One morning, as I continued to lie in my listless state, I heard someone walk in. Through the mess of what was my hair, I saw a tall woman sit on the edge of my bed. When I heard her speak, I knew who it was—my older sister who had taken special care of me when I was a child.

"Hi, Gussie," she said ever so tenderly. "Here, I've got a cup of water for you." With all the strength I could muster, I sat up and looked at her. She smoothed back my hair and stroked my head. The tenderness of it aroused me.

She said, "I'm so sorry, Baby Sister." I was wafted back to when I was a child and she comforted me like a mother.

Eventually, I drank all the water from the tin cup, and I tried to smile. "I must look horrible."

"Yes, you do," my sister said with a gentle laugh. "In a little while, I'll help you get up and change your clothes."

That was the beginning of my resurrection, not to make light of the Good Lord's resurrection, but there were similarities. My sister stayed with me for three days. She helped me with the most basic tasks of life—eating, drinking water, and even making my way to the outhouse.

Then she said, "I got to be goin' now, Gussie. My husband and kids are waitin' for me. I'll come back when I can."

I told her I understood and thanked her from the bottom of my heart. Then she was gone. The house was quiet again.

*****

I wanted to keep the little house that John and I had made into a real home. When we first got married, I made curtains, a tablecloth, and a quilt for our bed, but I needed enough money to keep renting our home. I made one of the biggest decisions of my life. I quit school and started working as a laundress at a hotel. I had become my mother.

I could say I was stupid for marrying so young, but I've come to believe that you should give your all for love. True love comes so rarely. I don't regret marrying John and the wonderful—albeit short—time we had together. After John died, the survival of my daughter and myself was most important. My hopes and dreams for the future all but flew away. However, Fate had other things in store.

SIX

Clay was the only thing that mended my broken heart. Whenever I could, I went to the pit. I made a couple of animals. However, I now molded faces of people from my imagination—people whose spirits I had encountered. A man with angry eyes, a woman with delicate eyebrows, a baby with a half-smile, a young man with a happy grin. They were quick, small, almost abstract works, but making them gave me an outlet for my tangled emotions. I left them among a lump of branches and leaves by the creek. I knew my new role was to be a dutiful mother and provider.

I was surprised one evening when my youngest brother knocked on the door and told me that Daddy wanted all of his children to meet at my parents' house. He had something important to tell us. By now, there were nine of us left. Big and small, married and single, we all sat down on the floor in the front room and listened to Daddy.

"We need to be leaving Green Cove Springs," he announced firmly.

The little ones groaned, "Oh, no." A couple of them got tears in their eyes.

Daddy continued, "We gotta go to West Palm Beach."

"West Palm Beach?" one of my brothers asked like it was some kind of hell waiting to burn us all up.

"Where's that?" one of my older sisters asked.

My daddy looked at us with angry eyes. "I'll tell ya all where, if you quit bein' so out of order."

Not until we were all quiet did Daddy continue. "West Palm Beach is a couple hundred miles down south of us."

When we groaned again, Daddy said, "There's a reason for West Palm Beach, and again I'll explain if you listen!"

29

We quieted down.

"This is the problem. Green Cove Springs used to be the easiest warm place for the rich tourists to go to in the winter, and we have that spring water. Henry Flagler, that guy who built a couple of hotels in town, now's built railroad tracks goin' all the way down to Palm Beach. It's right on the ocean—which I hear the tourists love. So, the Whites are startin' to go there more than Green Cove Springs."

My one brother who always had a smart-aleck answer asked, "What do we care where the Whites are going?"

Daddy looked at him like he was crazy. "We care, because they're takin' their money with them. If the Whites don't come here no more, your mama and I are gonna be out of jobs. Remember we work for the hotels."

"Daddy, may I ask, how do you know all this?" one of my older sisters asked in a very polite way so as not to upset him.

"You know I paint rooms for the hotels. They ain't needed me so much lately. I asked my boss why, and he done told me all this."

My older sister who nursed me back to health said, "If you don't mind, Daddy, I think me and my family will stay here."

"That's okay," Daddy said. "You're grown. You grown ones can make your own decisions, but you young uns have to come with us."

All that Green Cove Springs held for me now was endless toil as a laundress and constant reminders of John. Palm Beach might not be better, but it probably wouldn't be worse. "Irene and I will go with you," I said. For the first time, I realized that if I'd never met John or had a child by him, I may have remained with my older siblings in Green Cove Springs. I would have never experienced what I did in West Palm Beach, and I probably would have never come up to New York City… for better or worse.

Even though I didn't think I had much of a future in Green Cove Springs, I couldn't believe we were leaving. I felt like I was walking around in a cloud. I would miss so much—my older sisters and brothers who decided to stay and keep the farm, the stream from the hot spring gurgling down to the St. John River, the old oak trees swathed in moss like scary ghosts, and our family's barnyard animals. But mostly I would miss my clay.

It was quite a journey from Green Cove Springs to West Palm Beach. Friends of my parents took us via horse-drawn wagons to the Florida East Coast Railroad Station in Jacksonville. Transporting all of us and our clothing and cookware called for about eight wagons, but this was the way Colored families helped each other back then down South.

Daddy had saved money for a whole year to buy a new horse and a roof for our house, but he used it instead for our train tickets.

None of us had ever been on a train before. With all of its roaring, squeaking and smoking, it looked like a gigantic monster. Irene's little body shook as she held tightly onto my hand.

When my older brother explained in a calm voice to all the young ones that the train was just made of steel and was powered by coal, they all seemed to settle down—even if they had no idea what he meant. Their faces turned from fear to wonderment.

However, in no time I became agitated for a different reason. We Colored folk could only sit in certain cars. Conductors assisted the White men and women—oh so respectfully—to their cars while they almost shoved us in the direction of our quarters. Once inside our car, I noticed the floor was dirty and the rows of seats were crooked. What my parents said years earlier about Jim Crow laws finally sunk in. Now I knew what it was to be treated like an inferior human being.

SEVEN

We were among the first families who moved to West Palm Beach for work. What was later called the Florida Everglades was right at our doorstep. That meant mosquitoes attacked us constantly and tried to suck out all our blood.

My parents got jobs immediately to work in the big hotels. There was a special housing development for the hotel workers. I wanted a place just for Irene and me. So, I used my last name "Moore." Much to my relief, the manager gave me a home a couple of houses down from my parents.

The homes for us workers were lined up in rows, each one only being about five feet from the other. Every house had a small window in the front and three windows on the sides. There was a narrow front porch and three stairs made from concrete blocks. Each house was maybe 40 feet long and 25 feet wide. This was enough room for my child and me, but it was crowded for my parents who had five of my sisters and brothers with them. I missed living on a big plot of land like we had in Green Cove Springs.

The Hotel Royal Poinciana and the Palm Beach Inn were the biggest hotels in town. Word was that the Hotel Royal Poinciana was one of the largest hotels in the world.

A few White people worked at the hotels, but they could live wherever they wanted. My mama and I got jobs as laundresses at The Palm Beach Inn. Daddy painted walls and did handyman work for them. He also became one of the preachers at the Methodist Church in our Colored area, an honor he did not take lightly.

Still wanting to do something special some day, I made one of the best decisions of my life. I would go back to school. I'd continue working as a laundress, but wouldn't take too many hours. Entering my new school,

I would be eighteen years old, but people went to school when they could in those days. It wasn't uncommon.

The only catch was that I'd have to find someone to watch Irene. I talked it over with my mother, and we agreed that my older sister, who seemed happy staying home, would be a good one to ask. Thankfully, she agreed. My little girl seemed to like being at my Mama's and Daddy's most of the time anyhow.

Soon after we got to West Palm Beach, my daddy took me on an errand to Palm Beach. For the first time in my life, I saw an ocean. I feasted my eyes on the never-ending waters of blue. I marveled at the sound of the waves rolling into shore and clapping like thunder. I enjoyed the feeling of the ocean breeze as it kissed my cheeks. And I savored the taste of salt finding its way into my mouth.

I wished I could be a rich tourist able to enjoy the beach whenever I wanted. Whites sauntered up and down the walkways in fancy clothes or sat by the water with colorful parasols. Because of the color of their skin they could easily enjoy the good things of life—while we Coloreds worked like the slaves my grandparents once were.

On our buggy ride home, I voiced my grievance. "Why do those White people get to enjoy the beach and we have to work so hard?"

Daddy rebuked me like I'd just said a string of bad words. In his most forceful minister manner, he said, "Hush now, Gussie. You don't know how blessed we are that we're not slaves anymore that can be bought and sold like my papa was!"

I was old enough to hold my own with my father. "It still isn't right," I answered with conviction.

Daddy didn't reprimand me. Instead he turned and stared at me. Maybe—deep down inside—he felt the same way.

The mosquitoes drove us crazy. Mama kept a small herb garden, and she insisted we rub the mint from her garden on our bodies to keep from being bit. I brought some mint home and made Irene rub it on her body. She'd cry and say, "Leave me alone."

I rubbed mint on myself as often as I remembered, and it helped somewhat. When we got bad bites, Mama said we'd be cured by rubbing basil or garlic on ourselves. We seldom accepted that cure.

What really irritated me, though, was the absence of clay in West Palm Beach. The dirt was dry, and there were no creeks. Although my mother was terribly busy, she noticed my misery. One day, she said, "Gussie, why you droopin' like that? You're not yourself."

"I miss my clay, Mama."

"That clay just got you in a heap of trouble with your daddy. You're better off without it."

"I'm a woman now, Mama. Daddy can't keep me from the clay anymore."

"I guess you're right there."

My saving grace was that I liked the school I attended. When our teacher, Miss Fields, had us read famous poems, I decided to write one of my own. I showed it to her, and Miss Fields said it moved her to tears. I soaked up praise like a sponge. In my family, praise was as rare as a Florida snowflake. Not that our parents didn't care, but they worked so hard to feed and clothe us, they didn't have the time or energy to notice what might be our special talents. Although Mama still told me on my leap year birthday I would someday do something special, her tone of voice said she wasn't so sure anymore.

I liked expressing myself through poetry, but I still missed my clay. Then, on a pretty spring day, good fortune came my way. Along with a student named Priscilla, I had helped Miss Fields clean our classroom after school. We were there for a whole hour. Principal McNabb came into the room and in his sweet voice said, "My, oh, my, Girls! It's getting late. All the other children have gone home. Let me take you in my buggy.

It's not good to walk so far alone." Priscilla and I gratefully accepted Principal McNabb's offer.

First, he dropped off Priscilla. Then, as we were going to my house, he took a way I'd never been. Suddenly I saw a sign that got my attention:

Perkins Pottery

Factory Open to the Public

Knowing pottery was made from clay, I shrieked to Principal McNabb, "Stop. Stop! I have to get out."

He reigned in his horse, and the buggy almost toppled over.

"My goodness," he said in his proper way, "Must you be so adamant, Augusta?"

I said, "Sorry, I didn't mean to be rude, but I must look at something here. Could you kindly wait for just five minutes?"

Huffing and puffing with aggravation, Principal McNabb nevertheless agreed to wait.

When I went into the factory, I didn't see anyone. So, I went through to the back. There before my eyes were buckets of clay and a long table with something I learned later was a potter's wheel.

As I stared in amazement, a man came out of a nearby shed and said, "Hello, Young Lady, can I help you?"

He was White, which scared me at first, but he had such a friendly smile that I readily told him about how I made clay figures back in Green Cove Springs. He encouraged me to dig my fingers into his clay. It was pure gray and firmer than our clay back home, but I loved it. It was like old times.

Mr. Perkins was nice enough to let me take some clay. In fact, he gave me a whole big bucketful and offered, "I'll be happy to give you more, but you must come back first and show me your art."

Art! I had never thought about my clay work in that way.

After Mr. Perkins gave me clay, Professor McNabb drove me home and, along the way, asked me a lot of questions about my clay work—my "art."

If I had never seen that pottery shop, I might still be living down South washing bed sheets.

*****

As soon as I could, I began sculpting my barnyard animals. However, I didn't want to let my precious clay harden. So, I kept splashing water over it to keep it moist. What I created and let dry would have to be special. I thought and thought about it. Then one day I saw a picture of Mary, the mother of Jesus. I got inspired. *Why not sculpt her?*

Behind my house, I rigged up a little table by putting a board over a bucket. I decided to make my sculpture show Mary from the waist up. It would be about a foot and a half tall, and it would be very simple. If my father came over and saw me working in clay again, I was prepared for him to smack my creation off the table...even if it depicted the mother of God. Luckily, though, he didn't notice. At least not until I was almost done. I vividly remembered the day I saw his shadow loom again from behind. I was ready to be defiant. After all, I was a full-grown woman. But Daddy was silent. He just stared at my Mary for a while, touched it, and said, "Gussie, this is beautiful. This isn't the work of an idolater. I'm proud of you."

Such praise coming from, of all people, my father! I felt like I died and went to heaven.

I decided to use my little remaining clay to sculpt a duck. I would give it to Mr. Perkins.

When he laid eyes on my little creation, he got excited. "This is beautiful, Gussie! It's so detailed and realistic."

I felt myself beaming.

Then he added, "I have a hunch you don't have any sculpting tools, though. Some of your details look a little rough around the edges."

"All I have is a kitchen knife and some twigs."

36

"I'll tell you what, Gussie. I'll let you have a few of my implements."

When he brought me into the part of the barn that he had converted into a workshop, he showed me his set of ten metal tools.

"Here, you take these," he said, as he handed me three.

"Oh, I can't, I can't…" I stuttered.

"Oh, yes, you can," he said with a big smile. "I have more, but if it makes you happy, I'll charge you a small amount for these. Just pay me a little at a time when you can. And, here, take another pail of clay. Come back for more when you need it."

"Thank you, thank you," I gushed, and I surprised myself by hugging Mr. Perkins. I had never come so close to a White man before.

Using those tools really improved my pieces. Eventually, I paid back Mr. Perkins, and later I bought additional tools that I carried with me wherever I sculpted.

One day I brought two of my clay pieces to school to show Miss Fields. She said, "Gussie, you are quite the talented girl. First, the poetry, now the gorgeous artwork!" She showed Principal McNabb one of my ducks. The next day he called me into his office and told me he would pay me a dollar a day if, in my last few months of senior year, I would teach the other kids how to model clay. "Dabbling in the arts is good for a young person," he declared.

This was when I began envisioning myself climbing a ladder or a staircase to success. I still didn't know what that success would be, but it sure looked like it would have something to do with what Mr. Perkins called art.

That night in my bed I thought about my new good fortune. I imagined every compliment as a step up. I wrote a poem:

I do not know where the stairs will lead
But there is something I firmly believe

When I climb up, I won't be a laundress
Those stairs will lead to a greater success.

The poem wasn't one of my best, but sometimes I just liked to write down what I felt.

I still missed John. We were so easy and comfortable together. He let me be whoever I wanted to be. Yet, at the age of about twenty, I remember looking in the mirror and feeling maybe it was time to move on.

In that mirror by my front door, I saw a pretty young woman with soft brown skin, almond-shaped eyes, and eyebrows that framed them just right. It was fine with me that my nose was a little wider than those of White girls I had seen. I was Colored and proud of it. My teeth protruded somewhat, but they were straight, and I regularly cleaned them with a coarse cloth and soap. My hair was fine-textured and frizzy, so I kept it short and pulled back, which emphasized what I thought were my pretty facial features. I turned left and then right and observed my strong, slim body.

Some girls might want to carry a little more weight to show they had money to buy all the food they wanted. However, I preferred being slim because that made it easier to get around and do things. It had been ages since I'd really studied myself in a mirror. I was happy with what I saw. Maybe I should have never looked at that mirror. Maybe I should have let myself look like a plain old washerwoman, but that wasn't me. I had too much life in me.

Maybe I should have never looked in that mirror. Maybe I should have lived like a nun, but that wasn't me.

On a cool December morning, I went into town with one of my brothers and set eyes on the man who would soon set my world to spinning. I saw him sitting in a shiny, black Model T parked on a side street. As we rode by his car in our humble buggy, the man called, "Hello there." He looked older than me and wore his hair all slicked back with pomade in the latest style. I thought, *He might be a little older, but he is good-looking.*

When we rode back the same way, he was still parked there and said, "Hi again. Can you folks stop for a minute?"

My brother pulled in the reigns, and the man said, "Hi, my name is James Savage. What brings you all here on this fine morning?"

I smiled at him. "We came to town to do some shopping."

"If you're ever back on this street, I hope to see you again. I wait for my boss here." He tipped his cap and said, "Have a nice day."

My brother said he ran across this man before and had heard about him. He told me how James Savage had a reputation as "a lady's man," but despite his going out with a lot of different girls, he never got hooked. Word was that he had high tastes in women and would only take the prettiest, most well-mannered one for a wife. Somehow I wanted to prove I had those qualities. I thought James Savage might be an interesting challenge. From then on, I made an effort to go with my family to Palm Beach so I could see him again sitting in his Model T. Eventually, I did. He asked me to go some place with him—to a house that had been made into a lounge.

When James came to get me, he was dressed in beige slacks and a white shirt with maroon suspenders. I wore a white blouse and red skirt with heeled sandals—all purchased with care from a resale shop in my neighborhood. Knowing that we looked good together, James and I swaggered more than walked into that lounge.

As the music played, I told James I didn't know how to dance. He asked me to join him in a drink so I could "loosen up." It was some kind of whiskey that made my eyes pop and my body tingle, but within a minute it did relax me. After I finished the drink, James got me out on the dance floor. He was so smooth that it was easy for me to follow him. After another drink, we moved together like one.

Later when James dropped me at home, I said, "I had a good time."

He leaned towards me and whispered, "You'll have some more good times, if you stick with me." Even though I was a mother, I was still young. The promise of excitement appealed to me.

The next time I saw him, James told me he was a chauffeur for a wealthy family. He started coming over whenever the family wasn't in need of their car. Little Irene would meet him at the door, and he would give her a piece of candy. Then he would take me and Irene around town in the Model T. I felt rich when we took those rides. James said he loved children and that if he ever got married, he could support his wife so she wouldn't have to work. Also, he told me how pretty I was. I fell for him. Within four months we got married. I invited him to move in with me at my little house on 916 Banyan Street in West Palm Beach.

After our marriage, I contemplated the meaning of my new last name: Savage. It was definitely a strong name. I thought of the way Whites seemed to see our ancestors in Africa—as savage beasts—uncontrollable and dangerous. Not a word that described James or that I'd want to describe me. My husband acted nothing like a savage...at first. He treated me like a queen, bringing me flowers and telling me that I was beautiful.

Within only two months after our marriage, I noticed changes in James. He had stopped smiling at Irene and giving her candy.

Although I quit doing laundry work for the hotel, James started dropping hints that maybe I should go back to work so we could afford nice things. He talked me into becoming the laundress for his employers.

Then James became temperamental. I always had food ready for him, because of his irregular work hours. When I had time, I would go out in the yard and work with my clay. He'd have to go through the back door sometimes to find me, and then he'd storm, "Whatcha doin' out there workin' with that dirty mud? Get in here, Gussie."

I was so shocked by what he said and how he said it that I came in and was all nice-like. John never talked to me like that.

"Do you have to do something so disgusting?" he'd ask at other times.

Meekly, I would explain, "But, James, I always have a bucket of water outside with a sponge handy to wash my hands."

"It's still not a decent way to spend your time."

Of course, I didn't see my clay creations as "dirty" or "disgusting." Sculpting was my passion. Also, I believed that maybe—just maybe—my clay work would lead to some kind of success, although it was getting harder to keep that dream alive.

I started listening for the Model T outside and quickly washing up and running inside before James came in. However, it was not in my nature to be submissive.

One day as we ate dinner I tried to reason very nicely with James. "Can't you understand what working with clay means to me? It gives me as much joy as you get from driving that car."

"Yeah, but it doesn't bring in any money, and it's dirty."

I spoke calmly and sweetly. "I told you I wash my hands when I'm done. And someday it may bring in money."

"I got to tell you, Gussie. My mama was a house servant in her day. She had to keep everything perfectly clean and neat. In the little shack where I lived as a child, she yelled at us if anything was out of place. When I laid eyes on you, I saw a pretty, well-kept young woman who took good care of herself. I thought for sure when we married you'd be like my mama, keepin' our house clean and neat."

I replied with what I thought was an understanding tone. "But, James, I do keep things clean and neat ..."

"Not perfectly," he interrupted.

"But pretty close to that. And with the clay..."

At that moment, Irene came banging through the front door. "Look, Mommy, I found this pretty feather on the ground."

I went to admire it.

Still sitting at the table, James said, "Now you got your daughter playing with dirty things."

All my efforts at understanding flew away. I stood up, walked towards James, picked up his plate of chitlins and threw it right into his face.

He stood up and yelled, "You no good..." He grabbed my arm and twisted it behind my back.

I screamed in pain. Irene cried and ran out the door. James kept saying cruel things like, "You're no kind of wife. You ought to be cookin' and cleanin' all day, you lazy no good!" I tried to wrench my arm free. Suddenly my father loomed large and foreboding at the doorway. "Don't you ever touch my daughter like that again!"

He went up to James, grabbed him by his fancy white chauffeur's shirt and demanded, "Understand?"

Like he was giving one of his most forceful fire and brimstone sermons, Daddy scolded James. "The Bible says, 'Husbands, live with your wives in an understanding way, showing honor to the woman as the weaker vessel.'"

When Daddy let go of his shirt, James grabbed his coat and ran out the door.

Shaking from James' rough treatment, I said in a feeble voice, "Daddy, thank you so much." My father had never taken my side before.

He didn't say another word. Daddy just turned around and walked out the door.

After he left, I was seized by an uncontrollable urge to destroy things. Anything to get rid of the fury I felt deep inside. I threw a pan against the wall. I kicked over a basket. Then I picked up the basket and threw it across the room. I got a metal spoon and whacked it again and again with all my might against the stove. All the while, I yelled out profane words.

I don't know how long I went on like this. For five or fifty minutes? I wore myself out. I collapsed on our kitchen chair and put my head in my hands.

When I was a child, I saw a woman in the fields acting strangely. She was yelling at the air, shaking her fists, and pulling out her hair. I couldn't understand why anyone would do that. Now I understood.

I yelled, "God, I know I'm acting like a mad woman, but why? Why me, God? Why did you take my beloved John and then give me this terrible James!"

Although I yelled at God, I knew marrying James was not His fault.

Eventually I calmed down. I put things back into order. The only remaining evidence of my madness was a small dent in the stove. James returned home. He brought me a bouquet of flowers and told me he was sorry. I didn't know what to do. None of my brothers and sisters had "put out" their spouses. I took James back.

From that day forward, we I didn't talk much. I kept sculpting. Although I listened for James' Model T, I took my time coming in the house.

The end for us came in a way I would never have expected. It started with a sign in town: "County Fair in six months. Submit artwork for display and awards to Mr. George Currie, lawyer, Palm Beach."

I found out from Mr. Perkins where Mr. Currie's office was.

Ever since my father saved me from my husband, I felt like he cared about me. So, I asked him if he would take me to Mr. Currie's, and I was honest about why.

Daddy still wasn't thrilled with my art, but after my sculpture of Mary, he wasn't opposed. He sighed and said, "I'll take you."

Seeing as how all the rich people in Palm Beach had automobiles, I knew we'd be out of place, as usual, in our horse and wagon. I swallowed my pride, packed six of my clay animals in a picnic basket, put a cloth over them, and went with Daddy to Mr. Currie's address.

The lawyer's office was in a fancy building with lots of white columns and stairs leading to two massive doors. When I entered, I sheepishly approached a lady at the front desk. She frowned at me, probably wondering what a girl like me was doing there. After I inquired as to exactly where Mr. Currie's office was, she half-heartedly motioned to a room down the hall.

The office door was partially open. I walked in, shaking like a leaf. Two men sat behind fancy desks.

"I would like to speak with Mr. Currie, please," I said.

"I am he," said Mr. Currie. He was a slender man who had an accepting face and the smile of a person with a cheerful attitude. After he introduced me to a scowling man who he said was his law partner, Mr. Currie motioned for me to sit down.

I was so nervous I could hardly get out my words, but somehow I explained why I was there. Then I pulled back the cloth to show him my little sculptures. Mr. Currie stood up, walked around his desk, and gazed upon them.

"Why, these are beautiful, and so life-like. May I touch them?"

Then he told me about what the fair would be like. He added, "I will be honest with you, Mrs. Savage, we have rarely given a Colored person a booth at the fair—not that some aren't capable artists. But few have asked, and," he hesitated for about five seconds, "almost every person who attends is White."

With a bravado I didn't really feel, I said, "I don't care, Mr. Currie. I just want a chance to show my work."

Of course, his law partner could hardly keep from hearing our conversation. He looked up from

44

something he was writing, fake-coughed, frowned, and shook his head. Mr. Currie paid him no mind.

Sitting down again, Mr. Currie put a pencil to his lips and thought for a while. "I can see that your clay sculptures are of excellent quality. I will give you a booth for them at the fair."

I was so happy I could have kissed Mr. Currie. Instead I thanked him profusely. I just about ran down the hall of the fancy office building. When I got to our buggy and told my father of my good fortune, he said, "Let me look at those things you got in your basket." He held up one of my ducks and said ever so quietly, "Sorry, Gussie about the way I used to treat you." That was a turning point for Daddy and me.

*****

As the date of the fair approached, thinking of actually exhibiting my ducks and chickens frightened me. Mainly because of all the White people.

Surprisingly, though, the fair-goers were so entranced with my birds that they didn't seem to care about the color of my skin. I won a $25 prize and a special ribbon for the most original exhibit. When I added that to all the pieces I sold, I earned $175, an exorbitant amount of money for a poor, Colored woman from West Palm Beach. This confirmed to me that I had artistic talent. And something else happened: I began to feel that maybe White people weren't all against us.

Mr. Currie believed so much in my ability he asked me to sculpt a bust of him. I'll never forget how worried I was. What if my proportions were off? What if it didn't look like Mr. Currie? I used my worry to prepare. I sketched my daughter's head over and over again for as long as she would stay still.

Kind Mr. Currie gave me money to buy the clay. When the day came for me to begin, I had my father drop me off at the Curries' house. It was such a pretty two-story home painted all in white. Inside, the flowery wallpaper, patterned rugs, framed art and elegant furniture almost took my breath away.

When Mr. Currie began posing for me, it was difficult at first to look directly at him. I wondered if I'd always be so timid around White people. However, his eyes were kind, and he looked up and beyond me anyhow. I knew Mr. Currie had done a lot to establish Palm Beach as a prosperous community, and the way he stared off into the distance made me think he was envisioning the city's future. Although he struck a serious pose, he wore a serene smile as if he believed things would always turn out well. Like when I sculpted John, I felt it was most important to capture my sitter's personality.

It took about ten sittings for me to sculpt Mr. Currie. I put a cloth over his bust whenever I finished a session and made him promise not to peek. I was petrified when it came to the big unveiling! Mr. Currie had his wife come into the room. After I pulled off the cloth, they both smiled widely and agreed that it looked just like Mr. Currie.

"I think you looked into my husband's soul," Mrs. Currie said.

The praise dished out to me by the Curries was appreciated, but the butterflies in my stomach made it difficult to enjoy the refreshments.

As Mr. Currie spooned some sugar into his teacup, he said, "I give you credit, Augusta, for having the confidence and determination to enter the fair the way you did."

A young, Colored maid served us. As she walked out, she tried to catch my eye. She nodded first at the bust and then to me with a look that said, "Well done." In that fleeting moment, I hoped that whatever she wanted in life she would and could achieve, although the odds were not good for a Colored woman. I was one of the lucky ones.

Mr. Currie told me he was the poet laureate of Florida, and I shared that I loved writing poetry also. He said he wanted to dedicate a poem to me someday.

"That is very kind of you," I said, feeling so full of appreciation I thought my heart might burst.

During the time of the State Fair and my sculpting the bust, I was very busy, and my husband was not at all happy. One evening as we ate dinner I told him about how Mr. and Mrs. Currie loved the bust.

James said, "You really think you're something...you and your dirty fingernails."

Again my heart burst open with rage, and I lost all sense of reason. I stood up, picked up my side of the table and jerked it so that James' plate landed on his lap. James came towards me and grabbed the front of my dress. His eyes popped with fury, and mine did too. But, probably remembering my father, James let go. He fumed, "We're done. I'm leaving. I'll be back tomorrow for my clothes."

So, a State Fair—of all things—busted up our marriage. Thank goodness for that!

I was glad to get rid of James, but I became concerned with how I was losing my temper. This was the second time I had set James' food a flyin.' I hoped I wasn't living up to my last name.

EIGHT

Mr. Currie was so pleased with my bust that he had a suggestion. "Why don't you go up to Jacksonville and see if you can get commissions from rich Colored people to do their busts? People who have money love to have themselves immortalized in paintings or sculptures. I'll write a letter of introduction to some people I know there."

By now, my confidence had grown, and I thought I might as well try. My family said they would take care of Irene. Mr. Currie paid me a whole $100 for doing his bust. I took that money along with my earnings from the fair and bought a train ticket to Jacksonville. Then I went to call upon the wealthy, Colored people to whom Mr. Currie had written the letters. Knocking on their doors was nerve-wracking for a Colored woman who was more used to washing bed linens for rich people than carving their likeness.

Everyone was polite, but didn't want to take a chance with me because I had so little experience. One potential customer tried to be helpful. "I hear that Florida A and M College in Tallahassee is looking for good students."

The man said it was a college particularly for Coloreds, since our people couldn't go to White schools. I thought that was the school where my teacher, Mr. Johnson went. I loved teaching clay modeling to kids at my school in West Palm Beach. Maybe being a teacher—not an artist—would be the room at the top of my stairway to success.

I needed to write to my mother to make sure she would still take care of Irene, but I knew she would. She and Irene were like bread and butter. I figured I would grab a hold of this opportunity.

It happened that Florida A and M was starting the semester. They offered me tuition, room, and board, and I gladly accepted. I felt important going to college, but when I realized we could only teach reading, writing and arithmetic and I had to master Latin, I lost interest. The clay beckoned me, *Don't you miss the feeling of my soft substance bending to your every whim? Don't you long to make me into something wondrous?* I missed my sculpting even more than Irene, as terrible as that seemed.

Within a year, I quit.

I used the little money I had to take a train back down to West Palm Beach. I could hardly look into my parents' and Irene's eyes when they met me at the station. My mother tried to lighten my spirits. "At least, you tried, Gussie. You got further in school than anyone else in our family."

Irene hardly looked at me. I had been away for a year. Good mothers didn't do that.

Since I lost rights to my house when I left, I now had to live with my parents. I started doing laundry again—this time for the Hotel Royal Poinciana. Darkness enshrouded me like the caul that encased me when I was born. My life was worse than it was when I first came to West Palm Beach. At least then I had a place for just Irene and me. As I strained to wash the linens, I lamented, *This is demeaning. Maybe I should have stayed with teaching, even if it was boring.*

To find a little joy, I bought more clay from Mr. Perkins.

Eventually, I decided to go back to see Mr. Currie, hoping he could point me in another direction. I had written him when I was in Tallahassee about not getting any commissions and finally deciding to return home. When he saw me at his office door, he had me sit down and then announced, "I have another idea for you."

He encouraged me to go to New York City and meet with a noted sculptor named Solon Borglum. He said Mr. Borglum had a school there called The School of American Sculpture. He had met Mr. Borglum once, and he offered to write a letter of introduction for me.

"Solon is from a family of great sculptors," he said. "His brother and nephew are currently carving heads of our presidents into the side of Mount Rushmore."

I was impressed.

When Mr. Currie added, "I am sure Mr. Borglum would love having a student with your talent," I took the bait. If someone threw me a compliment, I was moist clay in their hands. I couldn't wait to pack my things.

But poverty was such a part of my life. It was like a living thing, trying to hold me down, hold me back. How could I break free of its clutches to get to New York City? *I must find a way,*

I decided to take as many hours as I could doing laundry for the hotel. My hands became old and shriveled-looking. Finally, I raised enough money for train fare. By now I was twenty-eight, and Irene was thirteen.

One evening as Irene was braiding her hair in front of my parents' little mirror, I took stock of my daughter. By now she was almost as tall as me. She had a husky, healthy build and tightly curled hair that she constantly groomed and filled with colorful barrettes.

I came up to her and said, "Irene, I've been offered a chance to study sculpture in New York City."

She turned and looked at me. "Really?" She stopped braiding. "I suppose you're gonna go on your own."

Half-heartedly, I said, "No. I'd like you to come too."

Irene looked at me and said, "I'd just be in the way." She looked back at the mirror and fiddled with her hair.

It took me a few seconds to say again, "Oh, no, I'd like you to come," but my voice lacked enthusiasm.

Irene's tone was sullen. It told me she knew how I really felt. "I think I'll stay back."

The night before I left for New York I wrote a poem for Mr. Currie:

MY SOUL'S GETHSEMANE

At the forks of life's high road
Alone I stand,
And the hour of my temptation
is at hand,
In my soul's Gethsemane
I still have your faith in me,
And it strengthens me
to know you understand.

The poem was a little dramatic, but leaving my family in West Palm Beach was scary, and I was tempted to give up on my New York dreams. Knowing how much Mr. Currie believed in me made me persist.

It was 1921, and lots of people from Florida were going North. I chose to believe that life in New York City would be full of money and opportunity. Those who were brave enough to make the journey sent letters home bragging that the streets were paved with gold. I knew they exaggerated, but there had to be more of a chance for success in New York City than in West Palm Beach.

My mother and father took me to the train station, and Irene came too.

Daddy said, "God bless you, Gussie." I thought I saw a tear in his eye. Maybe he thought he'd never see me again.

With tears leaking down her face, Mama said, "You're so brave, Gussie." Then she gave me a hanky in which she had wrapped three silver dollars—not easy for her to come by.

Irene simply said, "Goodbye." She stood still as a stone. No outstretched arms. I forced a small hug on her anyhow.

En route to The Promised Land, I had to transfer a couple times. I couldn't believe all the Colored people on the trains. In the South, of course, I had to sit in the Coloreds Only cars. They were at the front of the train where coal from the steam engines spewed out cinders through the windows kept open due to the heat. The area for White people was in the last cars so those delicate passengers wouldn't have to put up with the cinders. By all means, protect our Whites and let the Coloreds suffer. I felt myself dripping with sarcasm along with perspiration. Nevertheless, my enthusiasm for the future far surpassed any passing feelings of bitterness.

Part Two

NINE

Once we got further north, there weren't any Jim
Crow laws. I could sit where I wanted, although I
usually chose to sit with my own kind. When strangers
sat next to each other they often struck up a
conversation, but this didn't happen between Whites and
Coloreds. We did everything we could to avoid each
other. Arriving in New York, I got directions at the
information counter to the address for Solon Borglum's
school on Forty-fifth Street. The tall buildings, busy
streets, and closely packed crowds both frightened and
fascinated me. The soot and smoke were reminders that I
wasn't breathing Florida air.

The address for Mr. Borglum's studio was
within walking distance of the train. Visiting Mr. Currie
in his fancy building gave me more confidence than I
would have otherwise. When I entered Mr. Borglum's
building, I inquired as to where his school was. For the
first time, I went up in an elevator. My stomach dropped,
and the screeching and thumping of the door's opening
and closing made my ears ring. The door to Mr.
Borglum's studio was open, and when I walked in, I saw
a large, light-filled room. Several young women and
men stood by their works in progress. A man whom I
assumed was Mr. Borglum wore a white coat and was
explaining something to a student. When he noticed me,
his attitude was not nearly as friendly as that of Mr.
Currie. I thought, *I'm in trouble. I came all this way for
nothing.*

Solon Borglum was slim and wore a suit under his white coat. When I handed him Mr. Currie's letter of recommendation, he studied it closely. "It sounds as if you have some talent, Miss Savage. I would like to take you on, but according to Mr. Currie's note, you have lots of talent but little money. I am sorry to say that only the children of the rich and famous work under me, and they pay immense fees."

Probably noticing how I winced, he continued, "But I have an idea for you. Cooper Union is an excellent school nearby with sculpture classes, and they give free tuition to all who qualify."

Mr. Borglum had a word of warning, though. "Don't get your hopes up too high. You have to show extreme artistic talent."

"I believe in my work," I said quietly.

"I will give you my card and write a note on it recommending you to the registrar, Miss Kate Reynolds, so she will consider you."

I breathed a sigh of relief. Then I added, "But can you recommend, kind Sir, where I should stay?"

He seemed to study me. "There may be some places to rent near 135th St., not too far away, where you might feel comfortable. Go to the train station, and you can take a trolley to 135th in Harlem." He paused for a moment and said very seriously, "Good luck."

When I got to Grand Central, I asked again for information. I was directed to what I was told was a trolley—a long car on tracks that had poles on top attached to a long horizontal metal rod. My heart skipped a beat. This was all so new to me. When I got in, I didn't know what to expect, but aside from some screeching noises, the trolley ride was smooth.

As I sat there, I thought about my interview with Mr. Borglum. I was disappointed that he wouldn't take me on, but at least he told me about Cooper Union; that could be a blessing.

Peering out the window, I observed my new surroundings. At first, I saw more fancy, tall buildings, and White men with business suits and a sprinkling of well-dressed White ladies. After about a half hour, the city looked different. Now there were four-story buildings squashed in right next to each other. White, bearded men wearing broad-brimmed hats and black suits walked briskly down the streets. The women wore long black dresses and white blouses, and their children dressed like smaller versions of the adults. I later learned this was where the Jewish people lived.

Then came the area where Mr. Borglum probably felt I would feel most "comfortable." Of course, it was the Colored neighborhood. Separate but equal like in the South. Getting off the trolley at 135th St., I found myself at a wide thoroughfare. The road was full of horses and buggies as well as automobiles. Storefronts—most with homemade signs—advertised all kinds of things for sale. I couldn't see where I could rent a place on this busy street, so I turned onto a side street. The brick buildings were about sixty feet tall and right next to each other. This was all so different from my surroundings in Florida! Children jumped rope and darted back and forth in games of tag. Adults sat on the front steps. Groups of men stood talking.

I saw a sign on a building that said Short Term or Long Term Furnished And Unfurnished Apartments. That was a big mouthful. I was glad I could read so well. I walked up about six steps, opened the outside door and entered the unlocked, partially open door of a little office on the first floor. A tired-looking lady greeted me with little emotion and had me climb three flights of stairs with her. The peeling paint in the hallway was a grimy beige. By the time we reached the third floor, I was breathing heavily. It had been a long, hard day. The lady drearily announced, "Here we are." She opened the door, and we entered a room with more peeling paint, a scraped-up wooden floor and a light bulb dangling from the ceiling. The lady surprised me by pulling out a bed from a wall. I'd never seen such a thing. In this single room, there was also a little sink and stove along with a chipped porcelain-topped kitchen table, two chairs and a couch with stuffing popping out. The rent was only $5 a month. It would have to do for now.

The next morning I got on the trolley going the opposite direction and asked the driver to please let me know when we got close to Cooper Union. I sat right behind him. As he left me off, the kind gentleman told me how to walk to the school. I was thankful to him and anyone else who helped me in this gigantic, frightening city.

Cooper Union was an impressive brick building with massive arched windows on each of its several stories. I found my way to a half-opened door that said, "Miss Reynolds, Registrar."

I peeked in.

Miss Reynolds groaned, "Come in." Sitting behind a big desk and poring over lots of papers, she looked at me like I was one big bother.

After hearing my plea for admission and reviewing Mr. Borglum's recommendation, she asked, "Do you have a sample of your sculpture to show me?"

I stuttered, "No, no, I didn't know…"

"The deadline for applications is tomorrow. The only reason I'm talking with you at this late date is that I respect Mr. Borglum and any recommendation he sends. However, if we don't have a piece of work whereby to judge new students by tomorrow, we cannot accept them."

A tear rolled down my cheek quicker than I could wipe it away.

Miss Reynolds looked sorry but aggravated at the same time.

Not giving up, I asked, "How about if I make up a sculpture by tomorrow?"

"That sounds impossible."

"If you could be so kind, Ma'am, as to give me some clay, I will do it."

Like it was killing her to make the effort, Miss Reynolds stood up and lumbered down the hallway, returning with a bundle. She was a large woman in height and weight and looked like she never did any physical work. I rushed to help her with the bundle.

She frowned. "I usually am not the one who has to carry these heavy articles, but here's your clay and a few sculpting tools. I even included an armature and board for you to put the bust on."

"Armature?" I asked.

A long sigh came from Miss Reynolds. "It's like a vertical support that you can put the clay around."

"Oh, yes, that!" I acted like I already knew and somehow forgot.

Thanks bubbled from me like water gurgling from the sulphur spring back home.

"That's enough," Miss Reynolds said. "Just make my effort worth it."

I might have been slender, but my arm muscles were strong, and my spirits soared. I carried that bag of clay with the armature like it was as light as a feather. When I got off the trolley, I started walking to my new temporary home. The sun was setting, but, as usual, people lingered outside on the steps and sidewalk. A nice-looking man, probably in his forties, sat on the steps talking to some kids. I decided to rest my hopes on him.

"How do you do, Sir? I am new in the building, and am trying to get into the Cooper Union School. I need to sculpt someone's head by tomorrow to present to the school. I know this is asking a lot. I don't even know you, but would you be so kind as to pose for me?"

The man laughed a deep, hearty laugh. "I'll be darned. That's the first time, and I'm sure it'll be the last I'll be asked such a question. Let me go in and ask my wife."

He came out a couple minutes later and said she didn't mind.

Thinking it wouldn't be right to ask him to pose at my apartment, I asked, "Could I possibly do it at your place?"

He laughed again and said, "Okay, let me eat some dinner first. Then come to apartment 3 on the first floor."

I went to my room. In about an hour, I took the clay to the sink, moistened it and brought it downstairs wrapped in a towel. The man's wife met me at the door and was as friendly as could be. When I walked in, the sounds of a lively bunch of kids set my ears to ringing.

The man came out of the kitchen licking his fingers from what I supposed was his dinner. "Welcome. This is my wife, Lucy, here, and I am Titus."

"I'm sorry we have only two chairs. We have mattresses in the kids' rooms and ours where we sit at times. We just came up from Mississippi," said Lucy.

I felt comfortable with these people and responded, "I guess you were told too that the streets here are lined with gold."

"We sure were," Titus half-laughed and half-scowled. "We've been here three months now. I was a minister and worked in the cotton fields back home. I'm trying to get work anywhere…especially at the docks… but everyone in Harlem wants those jobs…that's all we Colored men are given."

"I do ironing at a laundry," said Lucy, "and those heavy irons kill me."

"I hate it here," Titus said, "but I'll feel like a failure if I go back down South."

"Where you from, Gussie?" asked Lucy. "Everyone around here comes from somewhere else."

"I'm from Florida."

"Do ya miss it?"

"To tell you the truth, every second since I've been here, I've tried so hard to make it that I haven't had time to think about home." Home. Even saying the word made me lonely.

Titus looked worried about me. He said, "You can always visit with us, but I guess we better get goin' with this statue you're gonna make."

I looked around. Since I didn't see a table, I said, "How about if I put this clay on the ledge here between the two rooms? I'd appreciate it if you would stand a few feet away to pose. I'm just going to sculpt your head."

Titus stood as still as a statue. I got out my clay and started sculpting. After an hour, my legs and arms hurt. I knew Titus must have been suffering.

"I'm just about done. I can put on the finishing touches in my apartment," I said.

When I said he could finally move, Titus rolled his head around and shook out his arms and shoulders. Lucy came in from the kitchen. The kids crowded around. Although I needed to complete the details, the clay bust looked like Titus. There was no doubt that I had copied him well. Most importantly, I think I captured the look of a man who had suffered, but still retained his dignity.

The whole family loved Titus' bust, and I said I would give it to them after I showed it to Miss Reynolds.

"Thank you, thank you," said Titus and Lucy as they each put an arm around me.

As I climbed the stairs, Lucy hollered up, "Now that we're in the same building, don't be a stranger! Come and visit or borrow what you need. We don't have much, but maybe we can help."

The next morning I carried the bust on the trolley to Cooper Union. I had on the same dress that I wore the day before. Now streaks of clay covered it and decorated my fingernails. I had been up all night flushing out the details.

Miss Reynolds looked at me with scornful eyes. I must have been a sight to behold. Then she pulled back the cloth, barely touching it with her fingertips.

"Oooh!" she exclaimed. She stared into Titus' face. "He looks so real!"

She looked at me for the first time with regard. "You definitely have talent. As registrar, I've never made such a quick decision before, but I will admit you to our

59

four-year sculpture program at Cooper Union that starts in two weeks. I'd like you to leave the bust here for a while so I can show it to the instructors."

This was another White person I could have hugged. Instead, I said, "Thank you ever so much. You don't know what this means to me."

When I got back to my apartment building, Titus was sitting on the steps outside, and I told him the good news. He was happy for me but added, "I only wish I could find some work to do."

"I know you will, Titus, and thanks again for posing. I was very blessed to meet you and your wife yesterday. The school wants to keep your bust for a couple weeks, and then I'll give it to you."

"Glad to help," he said but still looked downcast.

I plodded up to my apartment and collapsed on my couch. Getting into Cooper Union was a dream come true, but now what would I do? My stomach talked to me and begged, *"Feed me, feed me."*

After I slept for a while, I went back outside. I remembered seeing a laundry out the trolley window. Not having money to keep paying for trolleys, I walked about a mile until I saw the sign, "Laundry" with a "Help Wanted" sign under it. I went in.

I had only met a Chinese person once before, but my impression was that the man at the desk was Chinese. He had a round-shaped face, very deep-set eyes, and a slightly yellowish skin.

He said, "Hello" and looked at me like he wondered what I wanted. Words tumbled from my mouth. He said, "My English no good. Please, slow down, Lady."

I spoke slowly and clearly, "I see you have a sign that says, 'Help Wanted.'"

"Oh, yes. You want job?"

"Yes," I smiled.

He motioned for me to come around the counter and pointed to several contraptions in the middle of the floor. He said, "These wash clothes."

When Mama and I did the family laundry back in Florida, we used large buckets to get water from the well, hauled the water to our house, boiled it in a big pot, added soap, rinsed the clothes, wrung them out by hand and dried them on a line. It took a full day to do one load of wash. At the hotels, we had large wash and rinse sinks, wringers, and lines to hang out the clothes, but it was still a big job.

The man pointed to one of the machines and explained how it operated through a few simple words and gestures. "See here—plug." He put his hand on a long cord coming out of the machine and placed it in the wall. Then he pointed to a button on the machine. "I push," he said, and when he pushed, I jumped. It sounded like a stampede of galloping horses.

He explained proudly, "New invention."

"Good, good," I said with a smile, showing him my approval of the thing. To myself, I thought: *That looks like an easy way to do laundry. I might not mind this job.*

Then he brought me behind a long row of clothes hanging on a rack, and, there, bent over four ironing boards, were four Colored women ironing shirts with the biggest, heaviest irons I had ever seen.

"That your job," he said.

I felt my face fall.

But I had to work so I could eat. "When do I begin?" I asked.

"Tomorrow at four o'clock."

I lugged myself back home. When I got to my apartment house, Lucy and Titus were sitting on the steps watching the kids play.

"Why so glum?" Lucy asked.

"Your husband may have shared the good news that I got into Cooper Union. They loved how he looked in that bust I made." Regardless of this good news, I probably looked sad, because Lucy asked, "But?"

"But I only get tuition. I have to work to pay for an apartment and food. I went over to a laundry, and the man hired me." I let out a long, sad sigh. "I have to do ironing."

"Join the crowd," Lucy frowned in sympathy. Then in a more cheery tone, she asked, "Say, why don't you eat dinner with us tonight? We're only having chicken foot soup, but it'll tide you over."

Both Titus and Lucy were all skin, bones, and muscle. Not an ounce of fat on them. That's what came from trying to feed yourself and a large family on food like chicken foot soup.

I accepted the invitation from these generous people. I had no idea where my next meal would come from.

During orientation, Miss Reynolds told us all about the history of The Cooper Union School for the Advancement of Science and Art. She said it was established in 1859 by an inventor, industrialist and philanthropist named Peter Cooper. I wrote in my notes a quote she attributed to Mr. Cooper: "Education is the key not only to personal prosperity but to civic virtue and harmony." He made his school free to the working class and poor. Students could get an education in art, architecture, engineering, humanities or social sciences. There was no color bar; the founder demanded only "a willingness to learn and a commitment to excellence."

Hard work and a willingness to learn. Those values came easy to me. Considering my simple beginnings back in Green Cove Springs, I just hoped I was up to the academics.

Once the classes started, I was amazed to find that I did well. I discovered that Mr. Johnson and Miss Fields had given me a firm foundation.

At Cooper Union, my art teachers taught us how to cast our sculptures in plaster. It was a meticulous process, but one that gave our pieces a very smooth surface, especially when used with tools to get rid of little bumps or imperfections. The teachers told us that someday our works might be immortalized in bronze, but in the meantime they showed us how to cover the plaster with brown paint or a solution containing shoe polish to create a similar effect.

With the other students, I was pleasant but reserved. Maybe that had something to do with my being the only Negro in the school, but maybe, too, it was from my desire to put all my energy into my art. Looking back, I know I was too independent for my own good. If only I would have shared more "the ups and downs" of my life with a friend or two. But the fact that other students and teachers complimented me on my sculpting was the most important thing to me at the time. With their praise, I felt I was climbing that staircase to success again.

Unfortunately, though, Poverty still held me in its grip. Even though I worked for hours at the laundry, my wages barely paid for my apartment and food. Hunger constantly threatened my strength.

TEN

In February of 1922, Miss Reynolds called me to her office. Quaking, I didn't know what to expect. She looked over her frameless reading glasses and said, "You have lost weight since you started school...a lot of weight...not that you weren't already slender."

My heart fluttered with fear. *Where is this going?* I wondered.

She went on, "We have never seen such a hard-working, gifted young lady at this school before. I called together an emergency meeting of the Advisory Council to see if, for the first time ever, they would vote to supply someone—namely you—money for room, food and transportation."

I could feel my eyes open wide in amazement.

Although physical affection did not come naturally, I was so overwhelmed that I looked for a way to thank my benefactor. I put my hand across the desk. Miss Reynolds took it, squeezed it, and said, "They voted yes. You deserve it."

Now that I had a bit more money, I cut down my hours at the laundry. I could also move. I wanted better than my shabby one-room apartment with toilet and shower down the hall.

The bad thing about moving would be leaving Lucy and Titus. They were so good to me. However, they'd been saying they might move back down South, as embarrassing as they thought it might be. I went to their apartment to share the good news, but no one answered my knock. Not one of their kids had been out front either. Oh, well, I would try again.

I found a third floor apartment at 228 W. 138tth St. It had two very small bedrooms and its own toilet and shower. However, just like with the last place, fingerprints and grime covered everything from the dark hallways to the banisters to the doors to the apartment walls. In the living room, the plaid pattern of a fake rug was wearing off from the wooden floor. The bathroom faucet dripped, and the paint was peeling. By now, I had learned that the landlords loved to collect high rents from us Coloreds and immigrants, but they didn't use the money to pay for cleaning or repairs. People said the buildings we were forced to live in had a name—tenements. It was a bad name to me.

Light came only from the windows in front and back of the apartment and from hanging bulbs in each room. Being an artist, I would have preferred much more natural light, but I decided to take the apartment anyhow. I liked that it had its own bathroom and two bedrooms, even if they were dingy and small. Furthermore, I was told there was a beautiful, large library only blocks away. I figured I would spend most of my time at Cooper Union, the library, and work. Within a few years, I told myself I'd be making enough money to afford a better place.

I felt my life finally settling into a comfortable routine. Mr. Kim even promoted me to working with the washing machines.

One night I had a dream. In it, I was standing in a large room full of pedestals topped with bronzed busts. One was my portrait of Titus. Another was my bust of Mr. Currie. A third was the bust of a boy who I didn't recognize (later, I realized it was *Gamin*). The other busts were all of beautiful Colored people. Shadowy spectators looked on in amazement. Miss Reynolds appeared and handed me a stack of money.

When I woke up, I felt like the dream was telling me what my future success would look like. My destiny was to become a successful artist—one who sculpted my people. My works would be a type of graven images—clay shaped and engraved with the features of my Colored brothers and sisters.The best part was that in my dream many admired my subjects' features and paid high prices for my work.

Usually my dreams—probably like other people's—had been scary, but this one got me up and going with a bounce in my step. Mama would have said the dream shouldn't have been a surprise. After all, being born on February 29th, enclosed in a caul, made success a sure thing.

On Saturday mornings my treat was to visit the 135th St. Harlem Library. At other times I popped in and out for short periods, but on Saturdays I let myself study its art history books to my heart's content. The works of Michelangelo and the classical Renaissance sculptors impressed me the most. I admired the way they depicted people in all different positions, glorified the human body, and gave their subjects an air of dignity.

I also enjoyed reading Shakespeare's sonnets, and I committed some of them to memory. Now and then I composed my own poems.

All this time I was very independent, just like when I was a child. I was proud of accomplishing so much on my own—coming up from Florida, adjusting to the big city, going to college, etc. but sometimes I was lonely. By now Titus and Lucy had moved. They had sent one of their older sons to my apartment with the Titus bust. The young man said, "My folks say they'll miss you, Miss Savage. They couldn't carry this big bust back to Mississippi, but they said to remember them whenever you look at it."

I still mingled with the students at school even though I didn't get close to anyone. Wanting to fit in, I pretended I was their age and told them about "my younger sister" Irene who might come to live with me someday. I never told them I was married...even though on paper only.

Irene and I exchanged letters about once a month. All seemed to be going well with her, my parents and the rest of the family, but then I received an alarming letter. My daughter told me she was getting tired of life in West Palm Beach. "It's so boring," she wrote. "New York City would be more exciting."

Although I wanted to have Irene with me again, I didn't know how I would supervise or support her. I was so busy and poor.

Thankfully, she didn't bring this up again.

ELEVEN

I was thirty years old and close to graduation when I found out about a wonderful opportunity to go to a summer art school sponsored by the French government in Fontainebleau, outside Paris. One hundred American women were to be selected by a committee of well-known American artists. The tuition was free, but $500 for living expenses would be needed. I worked extra hours at the laundry to come up with the $35 application fee. After I submitted the fee, I was accepted, and joy filled my heart.

People who knew of my work volunteered to give me money towards the $500 for living expenses. I needed two references, but before I could get them, I received a letter saying my $35 was returned "with regret." The Americans helping to arrange the trip didn't realize I was a Colored. They believed the White girls would feel too uncomfortable if they had to travel on a ship with a Colored girl.

Just like when I got so mad at James, I lost all control. I took the cups in my kitchen and threw them against the wall. I pounded my hand on the table. I screamed bloody murder, but no intelligible words came out. The tenant below knocked on my floor with a broom handle. This jarred me back to my senses—somewhat.

My mind told me I didn't want to destroy the little I had. It told me instead to take my bathroom towels and wring them out like I was doing laundry. I would have preferred to wring the necks of those prejudiced people who blocked the greatest opportunity of my life. As I strangled the life out of those towels, my mind told me something else; I was living up to my name: "Savage." But I didn't care.

I couldn't sleep all night. The next day I ran to Miss Reynolds' office.

Seeing my state, Miss Reynolds closed her door and sat me down. "What's wrong?"

I told her the whole story, and she was almost as incensed as I. She said, "Let me think."

She sat pondering quietly and then said, "The Ethical Culture Society. That's who you need to contact."

"What's that?"

"They have an office on 64th St. and are made up of ministers and philosophers who believe everyone is equal. They use the term 'social justice,' and they advocate for people who are discriminated against."

"There really are people who care like that? Are they White or Colored?"

"They're White. Let me call them."

"Okay," I said. A ray of hope brightened my heart.

"Hello, Mr. Martin, this is Kate Reynolds..." She told the man my whole story. Then she said, "You can talk to Augusta yourself."

Talking with Mr. Martin, I liked the way the man was very angry on my behalf. He said he would contact the head of the Fontainebleau committee.

At home that evening I breathed a little easier. Whites weren't all bad. After all, a number of individual Whites whom I met during my life treated me with respect. I thought back to Mr. Currie, the fair-goers who bought my art, Mr. Borglum, and Miss Reynolds. Sadly, though, such White people seemed to be in the minority in America, the Fontainebleau Committee being a case in point.

Two days later Miss Reynolds got me out of sculpture class. Walking with more enthusiasm than usual, she said to me, "Mr. Martin is on the phone."

When I picked up the phone, Mr. Martin said, "Hello, Miss Savage. I spoke with an artist named Ernest Peixotto. I found out that he is the head of the

Fontainebleau Committee. Actually, he even has a home in Fontainebleau. He told me you didn't have the two references..."

"But I was getting the references."

"I know you were, and he admitted he knew that, too. He said frankly the committee felt this avoided a difficult situation for the 'southern girls' who were accepted. Since you would all have to eat together, sail on the same ship, and study in the same classes, they thought this would be embarrassing for them as well as you."

Mr. Martin sounded like he was accepting Mr. Peixotto's explanation. I interrupted. "That wouldn't be in the least embarrassing for me!"

"I made the same argument with Mr. Peixotto." Going back to his more forceful stance on my behalf, Mr. Martin said, "My next step is to contact the committee as a whole and get them to see how this is so unjust!"

Again, at least I felt that someone was standing up for me. I could keep Mr. Martin on that list of fair-minded White people.

Mr. Martin called me a week later and said he sent a fiery letter to every member of the committee among whom were Edwin Blashfield, President of the National Academy of Design, James Rogers, President of the Society of Beaux-Arts Architecture, and Hermon MacNeal, leader of the National Sculpture Society.

Wow! When he ticked off those names and their positions, I thought they were probably some of the top people in the art world. You would think such prominent people would realize that educating the next generation of artists would be more important than the color of one's skin. When they replied to Mr. Martin with short letters saying they still concurred on the committee's original decision, my hopes were dashed.

This became a big deal. Mr. Martin was probably the one who shared the story with the _Nation_ magazine which published an article on May 9, 1923 criticizing the committee saying it was unbelievable that such "intelligent and liberal" artists practiced racial discrimination.

Mr. Martin was incensed enough to take a ship all the way to France to get them to admit me. It was probably Mr. Peixotto who he saw, because he lived in Fontainebleau. But again the answer was "no."

More news and magazine articles followed. Leading scholars and Harlem ministers as well as Franz Boas, anthropologist at Columbia University, spoke against the committee.

On May 23, 1923, a reporter and photographer from *The New York World* came to interview me at Cooper Union. Miss Reynolds said I could talk with them in her office, and she left the room. I was a nervous wreck.

The reporter asked, "How do you feel about the Fontainebleau committee denying you of your opportunity to study art in France?"

I thought for a moment. "I don't know how to comment. Can you come back tomorrow? Then I will have something prepared for you."

When they came back the next day, I made a statement that the reporter quoted me word for word in *The New York World*:

"I don't care much for myself because I will get along all right here, but other and better Colored students might wish to apply sometime. This is the first year the school is open and I am the first Colored girl to apply. I don't like to see them establish a precedent...Democracy is a strange thing. My brother was good enough to be accepted in one of the regiments that saw service in France during the war, but it seems his sister is not good enough to be a guest of the country for which he fought...How am I to compete with other American artists if I am not to be given the same opportunity?"

People across the country took sides. Some got wind of my address. I started getting mail. There were supportive letters, but there were cruel letters, too. Some accused me of trying to play a trick on the Fontainebleau committee—trying to pass for White.

My complexion was on the light side when compared to that of someone like my father's, but I wasn't ashamed to be "a Colored" and would never pretend to be White. The first time I read a letter like that after a long day at school and the laundry, I felt anger well up in me, but I tried to be calm. My apartment couldn't handle another fit of my rage. I decided to ask Miss Reynolds the next day if I could use her phone to call the press.

Telling a reporter about the letter, I made this statement: "They seem to have the notion that I must be a mulatto or octoroon...Now I happen to be unmistakable, and that way is obviously out of the question. Isn't it rather odd that such people should always suppose that when a Colored girl gets a chance to develop her natural powers it must be that she will want to be White?" As the years passed, I continued to feel proud of making that point and wouldn't take it back for anything.

I had more supporters than critics, though, and some even wrote letters to President Harding. Yet I knew that Fontainebleau was over for me. My family back in West Palm Beach became aware of all the excitement. I have to admit I sent them an article or two. I felt important to be famous for a while, but I wished it would be for one of my sculptures and not the fight for equality I felt forced to take.

TWELVE

Irene was fifteen by then. In her latest letter, she told me she was proud of me and wanted to come to New York to help me through this rough time. That was a nice sentiment, but I figured she was just as likely looking for adventure in the big city. Getting her enrolled in school and making sure she had clothes and food would make me extremely busy and overworked—not to mention even more impoverished.

However, I reasoned that Irene could meet a need of mine that was not being fulfilled—someone to turn to. Maybe if I shared my feelings with someone I wouldn't throw things around when I got angry. Also, I'd left her behind too many times in the past. So, I mailed a letter back and invited Irene to come live with me.

When I first saw my daughter at the train station, she reminded me of her father. Although bigger in build than John, she had his walk, and when she came close to me, I saw his eyes in hers. Oh, how I wished the three of us could still be together! John always believed in my gift for sculpting. However, for a split second, I thought the unthinkable. If my beloved John wouldn't have died, I probably would have stayed with him in Green Cove Springs and would not have met Mr. Currie, who inspired me to become a sculptor. Fate had that strange way of stepping in.

As we took the trolley to my apartment, Irene gazed out the window with the same wide-eyed wonder I felt upon my arrival in New York City. The truth was, though, that I felt like I was sitting next to a stranger rather than my own flesh and blood. We had spent so little time together during her fifteen years.

Once she unpacked, I prepared her for something. "I know this may sound odd, Irene, but the students I attend school with are all White and younger.

To fit in, I told them I was just 22 and when I talked to them about you, I told them you're my younger sister."

"What? That's ridiculous. You couldn't admit I'm your daughter!" She gave me a look that could kill.

If I had been a real mother for her through the years, I might have gotten up next to her and said, "Wipe that look off your face."

Instead I raised my voice. "Didn't you hear what I just said? I did it to fit in."

She gave me one more evil look and then put her socks in the second-hand dresser I bought for her. "I heard you," Irene said with her back to me.

Again, I ignored this show of disrespect, since I hadn't yet earned the right to discipline her.

*****

I continued going to the 135th St. branch of the library. Sadie Peterson, one of the librarians, organized a poetry reading group, and she invited me to attend. At that first meeting, we introduced ourselves to each other. Some of the members were Countee Cullen, Eric Waldron, Langston Hughes, and Gwendolyn Bennett.

One other person—Zora Neale Hurston—said she didn't write poetry but she did write books. Everyone welcomed her to join the group anyhow. She said she researched the dialects of Colored people and wrote using those authentic dialects. At that first meeting of the poetry group, she read an excerpt from one of her books. I got homesick because the accents of the characters wafted me back to the voices of my people back in Green Cove Springs.

At every meeting, group members took turns reading snippets from their work. Once Countee Cullen read an excerpt from his poem, "From The Dark Tower":

We shall not always plant while others reap....
So in the dark we hide the heart that bleeds,
And wait, and tend our agonizing seeds.

When he finished, he turned to me and said, "Look at our poor Augusta here. When it came to Fontainebleau, she planted, but she sure didn't reap."

I felt my blood boil and said to myself more than anyone else, "I sure didn't."

Langston Hughes turned to the group and spoke, "We were born into a different era from our parents who said to White people, 'Yes, ma'am,' and 'Yes, sir,' with bowed heads of submission. We will no longer wait. Our time is now. We are the 'The New Negroes'".

We clapped as if we were at a rally, even though we sat at two tables in a quiet corner of the library. "The New Negroes." I had never heard that term before, but I heard it many times thereafter in our group.

More and more I found the term Negro being used instead of Colored, especially in sophisticated circles, and this library group was one very sophisticated circle. Over time, I figured out that while the members wanted to take up the cause of the oppressed, most were brought up by fortunate Negro families who had not suffered poverty and low status like my parents. Although I was slightly jealous of them, I liked what they had to say, and I felt special mingling with them.

At another meeting, Langston Hughes read one of his poems. I asked him later if I could copy it, because it so much captured my struggle to climb the ladder to success.

Mother to Son
Well, son, I'll tell you:
Life for me ain't been no crystal stair.
It's had tacks in it,
And splinters,
And boards torn up, And Places with no carpet
*   on the floor*
—Bare.
But all the time
I'se been a-climbin' on,
And reachin' landin's,

And turnin' corners,
And sometimes goin' in the dark
Where there ain't been no light.
So, boy, don't you turn back.
Don't you set down on the steps
"Cause you finds it kinder hard.
Don't you fall now—
For I'se still goin', honey,
I'se still climbin',
And life for me ain't been no crystal stair.

Over the years, I re-read my copy of that poem until the paper crumbled. It was my inspiration.

I'll never forget the meeting at the library that night. Another member of the group, Gwendolyn Bennett, wanted to read one of her poems. It gave us Negro women such an air of dignity that it brought tears to my eyes.

To A Dark Girl

I love you for your brownness,
And the rounded darkness of your breast,
I love you for the breaking sadness in your voice
And shadows where your wayward eyelids rest.

Something of old forgotten queen
Lurks in the lithe abandon of your walk
And something of the shackled slave
Sobs in the rhythm of your talk.

Oh, little brown girl, born for sorrow's mate
Keep all you have of queenliness,
Forgetting that you once were slave,
And let your full lips laugh at Fate!

Just as Gwendolyn finished the poem, a white guy popped out from behind the shelves. He looked harmless enough with a pencil behind his ear and a notebook in his hand. "Sorry to interrupt, but I heard your great poems, Miss Bennett and Mr. Hughes. Did I get your names right?"

Everyone looked confused and perturbed. The man had broken the mood. Langston merely nodded and said, "You got the names right."

The interrupter introduced himself to the group. "I'm Joe Gould, and I write for the _New York Evening Mail_. I am engaged in the most challenging, epic task ever."

"And what might that be?" I was foolish enough to ask. Foolish, because Joe took this question as a sign of deeper interest.

"Thank you for your question," he said with a wink in my direction. "I am writing what I call _An Oral History of Our Time_. I think we live in exciting times, and I am going to write down every word verbatim that our time's most outstanding people tell me. And you folks, right here in Harlem in your little group, seem to have important things to say. When I complete my book, it will be the longest one in history."

We all groaned at once.

"Do you mind if I listen in tonight?" Joe asked.

Rolling his eyes and frowning, Countee said, "You can sit in, but if you write down anything, we'll look at it, and if we don't like it, we'll destroy it."

Throughout the poetry meeting that night, Joe kept looking at me. _What have I done to deserve this?_ I thought.

In the meantime, I had only one more year left at Cooper Union. I was proud that my instructors had passed me through my first year's work in two weeks and my second year's in a month. My early sculpting education from the Green Cove Springs School of Clay Pits paid off. I'd be graduating in 1925 at the ripe old age of 33. However, with graduation only a year away, I worried about what I would do next. Luckily, a golden opportunity presented itself. It came from our librarian, Sadie Peterson.

Mrs. Peterson was a Negro also, although you could hardly tell, because she was so light-skinned. She wanted to make sure she had all kinds of writings by Negro authors and poets, and she made displays highlighting our people's works, saying they were definitely equal to the literary contributions of White people.

On one of the many Saturday afternoons when I had my head buried in an art history book, Mrs. Peterson approached me. "Miss Savage, I know you're a sculptor. You don't realize this, but I have been talking with the Friends of the Library to commission you to create a portrait bust of Dr. W.E.B. Du Bois. This would give us an opportunity to have a Negro artist create something for our library, and it would furnish us with the likeness of one of the greatest Negro thinkers of our time."

"Wow! I never met Dr. DuBois, but I know he wrote a newspaper article condemning the Fontainebleau decision. It will be a great honor to sculpt him. Thank you."

Not being able to concentrate any longer on my art history book, I just about ran home to tell Irene.

I couldn't help but gush. "Irene, I've made it. I got my first really big commission."

"Yeah, and what's it for?" she asked half-heartedly, as she braided her hair.

"It's for a bust of W.E.B. DuBois."

"Isn't he the one who organizes those marches of our people in fancy uniforms?"

"No, that's Marcus Garvey," I said.

"Oh, then I don't know who Mr. DuBois is," she said as she continued braiding. After a long silence, Irene added. "Congratulations, anyhow."

I couldn't blame Irene for not knowing about DuBois. I just knew a little about him from what the people in our poetry group said. Fontainebleau may have caused me to falter on my stairway to success, but this commission was a step back up.

As if it were yesterday, I remember the day when Mrs. Peterson had Dr. DuBois come to the library to meet me. He was a handsome, debonair, light-skinned Negro—probably about twenty years older than me—but with eyes that sparkled like a teenager's. Dressed in an expensive-looking suit with vest and bow tie, he came across as a real gentleman. He said, "It's an honor to meet you, Miss Savage. I admire you for taking the Fontainebleau experience as an opportunity to speak up for our people." He paused and frowned, "However, it had to be so disappointing to you not to study in Paris."

"Yes, it was, Dr. DuBois, but life goes on. Thank you for the newspaper article you wrote on my behalf. It is a pleasure meeting you."

Feeling instant trust in Dr. DuBois, I had him come to my apartment for the sittings while Irene was at school.

Although embarrassed by my cramped kitchen and nicked-up table, I had Dr. DuBois take a seat across from me, and I pulled out my sack of clay.

I delivered the little speech I had practiced the night before. "To sculpt you well, it won't be enough for me to just capture your physical features. I need to know who you are inside, what's in your soul. That might sound a little scary…"

"Oh, no," DuBois broke in. "I wouldn't expect any less, and I am happy to tell you what makes me tick, although at some point I'd like to learn more about you. I was quite impressed with how you challenged the Fontainebleau committee and didn't just let them have their way without a fight."

It made me feel good to know that this famous man had noticed. I responded, "I'll tell you more about me later, but for now I am just taking big clumps of clay to put on the armature. So, this is a good time for you to share whatever you'd like."

79

DuBois hesitated, seeming to give this some thought. "It's difficult to say exactly, but let me tell you first a little about my background. I was a professor at Atlanta University and am rather proud that I am the first Negro to obtain a Ph.d. from Harvard. In 1909, I helped found the NAACP. However, I also want to tell you about how, in an unexpected moment of chance, I saw something that changed my life. Maybe this will tell what matters most to me now."

The finger of fate had pointed again, I thought.

"It had to do with a Negro named Sam Hose. He was accused of murdering his employer after a heated argument. Hose had requested time off to visit his mother, who was ill. His boss threatened to kill him, and he pointed a gun at him. At the time, Hose was working with an axe in his hand. To keep from being shot, Hose threw the axe at his boss, and the boss died. Hose fled the scene and was eventually discovered by authorities. Newspapers reported that hundreds of people heard about this and would not let the authorities take Sam Hose to jail. The mob grabbed Sam Hose and took him to a place where they severed his hands, arms and feet. Then they doused him with kerosene, lynched him and burnt him up. They fought over the poor man's innards and leftover body parts. I was walking down the streets of Atlanta talking with a reporter about it when I happened to look into the window and saw the knuckles of Sam Hose."

Suddenly sick to my stomach, I could not go on sculpting. "Disgusting! Absolutely disgusting! Hearing that could make me hate all Whites! I can't believe that so many people participated in that and took his body parts for souvenirs."

DuBois still looked a little shaken himself, even though he'd probably relived the experience a hundred times. "I vowed that from then on I wouldn't just research and teach. I would try to do things to eliminate lynching. So, now I am writing for the NAACP newspaper and trying to get politicians to make a law against lynching."

This knowledge about DuBois helped me with my sculpting. Now I felt I knew what his facial features revealed. His uplifted chin showed his confidence. His wide open eyes radiated his steely determination and vision of a better future for us Negroes. His mouth curved in two directions—one side going up in the pleasure of living and the other going down with worry about our race.

Our discussion was interrupted when someone banged on the door and called, "Gussie, I hope you're comin' to my rent party tonight!"

I stood up and opened the door to Claudine, my neighbor downstairs. Claudine was always so full of energy despite her difficult circumstances—unmarried, living with four children in an apartment no larger than mine.

I answered, "I'll try to come. How much to get in?"

"Just ten cents," Claudine said. The way she said "just" was her typical saleswoman pitch.

"Okay, I'll see if my budget can manage it. Bye." I just about closed the door on poor Claudine. I guess I was being rude, but Claudine could talk an arm and leg off you, and I was busy.

When I returned to the kitchen, DuBois said, "I've heard about those rent parties."

More to myself than him, I murmured, "I hope I'm never desperate enough to have one."

"You're a young woman, Augusta. I imagine that going to a rent party could be a lot of fun."

"I'm not that young. I'm thirty-three. Got a late start going to college."

"Being in one's thirties is young, I can say as a man in my fifties. I hope you don't think I'm being out of order, but you look even younger than a woman in her thirties."

I always liked being thought of as younger than I was.

Then out of the blue Dr. DuBois asked, "So what are your plans for the future, Augusta?"

It was just the question that occasionally kept me up at night. "Of course, after I graduate, I'd like to continue being a sculptor. It was the gift God gave me."

"And, I'm sorry if I'm being too forward again, but do you think you can support yourself with this passion?"

A pang of fear shot through me. I answered honestly, "I don't know, but I do know that sculpting is what I need to do. Besides, my mother imbued in me her belief that I would do something special someday that would make the world take notice."

DuBois grinned and said, "I like your mother without even meeting her."

When we were almost done with the sessions, DuBois told me about what he seemed to think would solve the problems of the Negro in today's world. It was his Talented Tenth Theory. "I believe that if one out of ten Black men can become educated, and I mean classically educated, they can lead our race out of poverty and address some of our other problems."

At that point, I was concentrating on using my tools to complete his right ear and commented passively, "Oh, that's interesting." DuBois may have wished for me to get into more of a discussion with him about his theory, but I had work to do.

When I completed his bust, I immediately put a towel over it. He said, "Can't I see it?"

I smiled mysteriously. "No, not until the library unveiling."

Two weeks later, after the clay hardened, I brought the covered DuBois bust to the library for the unveiling reception. I wouldn't even let Mrs. Peterson see it until the big moment. Besides the members of our poetry group, about twenty people showed up. Even a reporter came to take pictures. The Friends of the Library served cookies and punch.

Dr. DuBois stood next to the bust and the pedestal on which it stood. When Mrs. Peterson dramatically pulled the cloth from the sculpture, everyone gasped. "It looks just like him!" everyone crowed. As he twirled his moustache, Dr. DuBois whispered to me, "You are indeed in The Talented Tenth, Miss Savage."

Of course, I was overjoyed with everyone's positive reaction. And the amount of money the library paid me—$200—was a windfall.

Irene came to the showing also. I had told my poetry group the truth—that she was my daughter. I had nothing to prove to them like I thought I did with the young students at Cooper Union. As soon as we got home, I let off steam. I mocked DuBois' compliment as I strutted around with my nose up in the air and chanted, "I'm in The Talented Tenth, The Talented Tenth."

Irene looked at me like I was crazy until I told her about DuBois' theory. I concluded with, "He's a very nice man and helped organize the NAACP to fight for equality for all the races, but I think he fixes too much on this Talented Tenth thing."

"Where does that leave the rest of us? I know I don't fit into the Tenth," Irene said.

I shook my head. "That's why I was just poking fun about it, but Dr. DuBois is a wonderful man..." my voice trailed off as I kicked off my shoes and plopped down on the couch. "It was such a lovely night. I felt appreciated."

Irene commented, "The bust sure looked like Dr. DuBois." As she took out her barrettes, she added, "I noticed a man. He was White, short, and wearing a messy suit. Even when Mrs. Peterson or Dr. DuBois talked, he kept staring at you."

Nonchalantly, I said, "Oh, him, Joe Gould. He's strange."

"He seems to like you, Mom."

That did not sit well with me. I grumbled, "Well, I definitely do not like him."

In a more upbeat tone, I said, "I'm glad you came tonight, Irene. It was nice to have family with me."

My daughter looked at me and smiled. This was one of our rare moments of closeness.

Then I added, "But you better get to bed. This was a late evening, and you have school tomorrow."

Lying in bed, I thought about the many compliments I'd received on that special night. Back then, praise seemed more important than food or water.

THIRTEEN

My successful DuBois sculpture led to other commissions. I was flattered when Sadie Peterson told me Marcus Garvey's secretary general came to the library asking about my work. I came to the library the next day to meet this secretary, Robert L. Poston.

I was attracted to the man immediately. Mr. Poston was tall, slender and clean-shaven. Dressed in a black suit with an open-collared white shirt, he appeared to be about twenty-five.

He put out his hand in greeting. "Hello, Miss Savage. I have heard so much about you."

I quaked at his touch and was at a loss for words. Mr. Poston filled in the space by explaining that Marcus Garvey wanted a bust to immortalize himself as the man who helped Negroes find their true home.

When I asked him what that was, he said, "Of course, Africa."

You couldn't live in Harlem and not know about all the things Marcus Garvey did. Already this year there were two Garvey parades. As Irene said, she had seen his parades herself in the short time she'd been in the city. Garvey and his followers dressed in ornate uniforms, and people lined the streets to see his army of Negroes. I wasn't sure what that was all about, but it seemed to have something to do with developing Negro pride.

I said I would consider doing Mr. Garvey's bust.

The next day Mr. Poston brought me to Garvey's apartment in Harlem. Despite the fancy uniform he wore in his parades, Garvey was attired in a traditional suit. The only decorations in his front room were a few small Egyptian and Asian sculptures.

85

Mr. Garvey invited me to sit in a chair next to his, and he asked Mr. Poston to remain. He said he wanted me to come to his place every Sunday morning (with Mr. Poston present) and would pay me $300 for the bust, if he liked it. I was thrilled for the opportunity and the big money.

Then Mr. Poston escorted me outside and said, "How about if I walk you home?"

Although I said, "That would be fine," I felt timid. It had been some time since I'd been alone with a handsome, young man.

After he walked me to my door, I didn't ask him in. However, I hoped he would continue to walk me all the way back and forth to Garvey's.

Sculpting Mr. Garvey was enlightening. When I wasn't working on his mouth, he told me about his campaign to help our people. He spoke in a very abrupt, rapid manner. Every word was packed with emotion but not one more than another. He spit out words like a machine gun. Never once did the man smile.

"Miss Savage, do you know what I am trying to do?"

"No, Sir." I couldn't help but call him sir. He spoke with such authority.

"I have traveled and read widely, and I know that except in Africa, Negro people have always been treated as inferior. Our only hope is to unite, raise money, and take ships back to our homeland."

I admired the man, but I wasn't so sure I wanted to live in Africa.

One night I went to a speech he gave at Madison Square Garden that drew thousands. His style of speaking was just like I'd experienced in his apartment, although he spoke louder for such a large audience. His machine-gun style drew in the people, and they cheered fervently. This helped me in my sculpting of his bust. He was like the Negro Moses, and I would make him full of fire and conviction.

86

Once when I was sculpting him, I got the nerve to ask, "Why do you have the parades and the uniforms?"

"First, let me explain that the uniforms are not military. They are worn by different sections of my group––the United Negro Improvement Association—to bring each unit a sense of solidarity and pride. You may have observed that men, women and children all have quite different uniforms. I have the parades to help our people realize how important they are and that they are soldiers fighting for the respect they deserve."

I cleared my throat but still spoke with trepidation to this formidable man. "I saw your last parade a couple months ago. Some people carried posters that said 'White man rules America, Black man shall rule Africa.'"

"Yes, that shows our mission."

"But I also saw ones like 'We won the war.' I heard you went a little bit into the White neighborhoods with that parade."

"Yes, and I imagine you're implying White people weren't too happy with the signs."

I nodded a *yes*.

Garvey said, "Number One, Whites should be happy if we all leave America, since they don't want us to live near them anyhow. And Number Two, who cares what they think?"

This conversation made me realize how intense Marcus Garvey was. I didn't agree with all his theories, but he entranced me with the way he talked.

Mr. Poston continued walking me back and forth to Garvey's. I began calling him Robert, and he called me Augusta. One morning I invited him up to my apartment. Irene had gone to church with a family in the building.

At first, I felt awkward. *Why did I ask him in? What would he think about our dilapidated dwelling?*

I tried to overcome my anxiety, though, because I wanted to get to know this man better.

I showed him around and brought Robert by Irene's room with its pink bedspread. I don't know why, but a lie spurted out of my mouth before I could contain it. "This is my little sister Irene's room. I brought her up from Florida." Why did I go back to lying about Irene? Was it because I didn't want Robert to know I was older than him?

Robert seemed impressed. "That was nice of you to bring her up to New York. Your place is definitely cleaner than mine. I'm a bad boy, always so busy with The Cause that I don't take time to clean up enough."

When I brought Robert into my bedroom where I had my sculptures on top of my dresser, he looked amazed. "Wow! Your sculptures are fantastic!"

Pointing to my bust of Titus, I said, "This fine gentleman posed for the bust that got me into Cooper Union. I wanted to give it back to him, but his family returned to Mississippi, and they couldn't carry it."

"Oh, you went to Cooper Union?" Robert asked, seeming impressed.

When we went back into the front room, I motioned for him to sit down on the couch. I sat at one end and he at the other. We talked about a variety of things—the weather, the war that just ended, the new fangled cars that were coming out.

I asked Robert if he'd like a glass of water. When he said, "Yes," I went to the kitchen and came back with a glass for each of us.

"You know a little about me. Now it's time for you to tell me a little about yourself, if you don't mind," I suggested with an encouraging smile.

"I was born in Kentucky. My father was a poet, writer and teacher. My parents believed fervently in education and sent me to Howard University. After graduation, I worked for a while as a reporter and editor for a paper in Detroit. Then I heard

88

about Garvey's Universal Negro Improvement Association and started sending him articles for his group's magazine. Garvey welcomed me to write what I thought. A Negro could never do that for a White newspaper."

I said, "I really admire Mr. Garvey and Dr. DuBois whom I also sculpted. It seems like both men dedicate their lives to improving things for our people."

"Well, you know Garvey doesn't agree at all with DuBois, and DuBois thinks Garvey's trying to solve our problems by running away from America."

I asked, "What do you think of DuBois' idea that 'The Talented Tenth' are the only ones who can lead us forward?"

Robert furrowed his brow. "I don't like it. It's snobbish. Garvey, for one, does not have the formal schooling that DuBois thinks is so necessary, but Garvey has educated himself through reading and traveling." He paused and then looked at me intently.

I told him about a lot of things. About how I was the child of parents who had been slaves as children. About how my mother was illiterate and my father learned to read from other ministers. About doing lots of laundry work—and still doing it—to survive.

He stopped me there, "But you are an up-and -coming artist. Almost everyone in America has heard about you—how you got selected to that French academy because your work was so good and then how the committee wouldn't allow you to go."

"When the newsmen interviewed me, I felt had to speak out against racial prejudice, especially when it came to the arts. I felt good about that, but now…" I hesitated before expressing my worst fear…"I am afraid the people who were on that committee will punish me for what I said. They were some of the top people in the art world."

Robert took his right hand from his lap and put it over the back of the sofa, touching my shoulder ever so slightly. "I certainly hope they won't, but I admire you for speaking out. You suffered, but you got people across the country to start understanding what it feels like being a Negro in America."

The longer we talked the closer I felt to Robert. His eyes were welcoming, almost hypnotic. I hardly ever revealed so much about myself to anyone.

Eventually, he said, "I better go. See you next Sunday."

me by surprise, but I didn't hold
t, I love you, too."
n the couch together, we kissed—
deeply and passionately.

left that morning, I felt all warm and
we were moving fast, but Robert and
t for each other. Now I had to tell him
Irene. Would that change his mind?
had I fell in love with a man she hadn't

uiet Sunday afternoon when Irene and I
me, I explained about my relationship
added, "Baby, Robert is just as sweet as
ohn Moore. I know you don't remember
oved you with all his heart, and he was
asses."

brought a tear to Irene's eyes. "You
talk about Daddy."
now. I guess it makes me sad when I think
miss him. I've tried to push it down."
h of us sat quietly for a while. Then I said,
ys been so busy with my laundry work and
that I've been able to ignore unhappy

Don't I know it!" Irene said in a voice
h anger.
You will like Robert," I said, getting back to
al conversation.
At least you told him the truth. I've just been
ecret since I came up here."
'I'm sorry, Irene. You know why I told the lie
er Union, but at least I told our poetry group
h." I wasn't going to tell her I lied to Robert
d confess the truth to him before I got the two
together.
And, so, two nights later I admitted to Robert
ene was my daughter. I told him I was afraid he
lose interest in me if he knew I was an older
n and had a grown daughter.

FOURTEEN

Harlem throbbed with life. More and more people came up from the South to rid themselves of the cruel Jim Crow laws. They wanted to make something of themselves, and I identified with them. Also, I started identifying with the people in our poetry group. Each had made a name for him or herself. I hadn't made my mark yet, but I felt sure I would. All in all, living in Harlem, I felt like I was on the cusp of the success my mother predicted.

However, the environment in Harlem was challenging, too. Since we Negroes weren't welcomed elsewhere in the city, Harlem literally burst at its seams. It got untidier by the day. The landlords kept letting the apartments deteriorate and, honestly, our people—having come from a rural environment—didn't seem to know how to keep them up. Like my family when we were in Green Cove Springs, they were used to living in simple wooden shacks and spending most of their time outdoors. If they had ten children, it was all right down South, because the kids helped with the work, and it was warm enough all year round for them to be outside. In Harlem the sidewalks were the only place the children could play. When it was freezing cold, having ten kids in one apartment was a challenge. If there was a stray pencil or crayon, the walls could become the children's tablets.

Yet I was inspired by the shining examples of people in Harlem who did make their dreams come true. Many were musically talented. I knew from experience how their musical interests evolved. Their parents, like mine, probably sang spirituals together in the fields.

This led to them being in the church choir and learning how to play piano. I heard that a couple of young Negro musicians named Louie Armstrong and Count Basie were making a hit in Harlem. Some entertainers put together big bands. White people, many of them rich, drove into Harlem to hear the music. My people developed a new kind of music called "jazz."

Most everyone in Harlem wanted a job, and we were willing to work hard, if we could actually get a job. I continued to work at the laundry to supplement my earnings from sculpting busts. Irene worked with me part-time in addition to going to school, but I let her keep much of the money she made. Like most young people, Irene had to have the latest thing. In her case, it was a new invention called the radio. When she bought a radio, I was as enthused as she to hear its music, comedies and news.

I realized that the radio was changing America and even the world. When it advertised certain types of clothing or appliances, everyone wanted them. I must admit I was one of the many who craved the things I could not afford.

Women in our neighborhood and in downtown Manhattan started dressing in new and different ways. The old style of long, dark dresses was gone. The new thing—especially for going out—was to wear a straight dress without a waistline that ended just below the knees. Along with these new-fangled dresses, women wore long fitted gloves, imitation or real pearl necklaces, and headbands with feathery accessories. Oh, how I wanted to dress like that!

The way our men were treated after the war had a big effect on them. Returning Negro soldiers thought they would be regarded with newfound respect. After all, they had lain in trenches and risked their lives just as much as any White men. However, they were still regarded as second-class citizens. My

broth
injust

the los
wanted
People
Charlesto
group can
radio afte
tunes. Irene
but we laug

Not
sometimes w
me—wanted
the town" on
kept me down
with the right
my little money
for Irene and me

Robert w
go from sculpti
bombastic talk ag
Robert. While he
Robert spoke quie
nothing too serious.

Every Sund
closer. One day, Ro
admit this, since we n
think…" he took a dee
I encouraged
Robert…what is it?"

"I think I'm fal
I've said it." He exhaled,
lifted from his shoulders.

He continued, "Yo
like it when you talk. You
smile lights a room, but y
your face clouds over with
want to take care of you. I wa

He took
back. "Oh, Rober
Sitting
first lightly, then
After he
hopeful. I knew
I seemed perfe
the truth abou
Would she be
even met?

On a
were both ho
with Robert.
your father, J
him, but he
sweet as mol
Tha
hardly ever
"I k
about how
Ea
"I've alwa
sculpting
feelings."
"
tinged wi
our origi
one big
at Coop
the trut
also. I
of then
that Ir
might
woma

Robert asked, "And how old do you think I am?"

"About twenty-five?"

He burst out laughing. "I am thirty-two years old."

I leaned back in shock and took a close look at him. "No! Then I'm just a year older than you."

After we both quit laughing, Robert said, "But don't you ever lie to me again, Augusta Savage." Thank goodness, he said it playfully as he gave me a little kiss.

"I've never lied about anything else in my life but this age thing. Oh, except for telling my parents I wasn't going to the clay pit when I really was. You don't have to worry about me lying again, I promise."

I told Robert all about my marriage to John and how he died. I didn't want to tell him about my marriage to James Savage, but I felt I needed to explain my last name. I didn't know how to tell him I never got a divorce from James. There was just never the money for it. Was failing to tell a person something the same as a lie? I hoped not.

I arranged for Robert to come over in the evening for dinner to meet Irene. He made Irene laugh when he told her the names of his siblings—Theodore Roosevelt Poston, Fred Douglass Poston and Ulysses Grant Poston. "My middle name is Lincoln," he added. Irene and I collapsed in laughter.

Slowly Robert drew out Irene, finding out details about her schoolteachers and friends, things she hadn't even told me. The evening was a success.

Robert and I moved fast after that. We decided to get married by a justice of the peace in just six weeks. I wrote to my parents about our decision.

Being in love made me tingle all over. Everything was special. The birds sang even more cheerfully, the sun shined brighter, people seemed nicer. Being embraced by Robert was the best part. I didn't have to be so independent anymore. I had someone to lean on.

But once we made definite marriage plans, Robert's tone changed. He was still very sweet and considerate, but he began talking more about his political beliefs. I couldn't help comparing him with John who never changed, who always enjoyed the simple things of life and didn't ponder the deeper meaning of it all. At least, Robert didn't become mean to me, like James did.

"I'm so disgusted with the White power structure, Gussie (he was one of the few people up North who I asked to use my Southern nickname). We will never have equal rights in this country. Just look at the Klu Klux Klan."

We complained vehemently about the sad situation of our country for a couple of hours on one Monday evening. Irene came out of her room. "Could you guys please be quiet? I'm trying to study."

A couple of days later Robert came over and was smiling with excitement. He said, "I am going to read a poem for you that I just wrote. I'll stand up to give it full effect."

Robert looked so handsome—jacketless, in his black slacks and form-fitting, white shirt. I had the feeling that he'd read me a love poem. Sad to say, it turned out to be far from that. His face turned serious. "The title of my poem is 'When You Meet a Member of the Klu Klux Klan'."

Robert's eyes became wide with emotion, and he moved his hands in dramatic gestures as he read from a piece of paper.

When you meet a member of the Ku Klux Klan,
Walk right up and hit him like a natural man;
Take no thought of babies he may have at home,
Sympathy's defamed when used upon his dome.

Call your wife and baby out
To see you have some fun,
Sic your bulldog on him to see the rascal run.
Head him off before he gets
Ten paces from your door.
Take a bat of sturdy oak and
Knock him down once more.
This time you may leave him
Where he wallows in the sand,
A spent and humble member of the Ku Klux Klan."

When Robert finished, he took a deep breath and sat down.

I was speechless.

"Well, what do you think?" he asked with a look of eager anticipation.

"It's rather violent," I said quietly. I didn't want to disagree with Robert, but I couldn't keep from frowning.

"I used the power of hyperbole," he tried to explain. "You look like you didn't approve of the poem, but, Gussie, we're never going to get anywhere if our people roll over when attacked."

I had to agree, but I still thought the poem was too harsh. Robert said he was publishing it in Garvey's newspaper. We never talked about that poem again.

A few weeks later we went to obtain our marriage license. During those few weeks I worried about what would happen if it was discovered that I was committing bigamy by marrying again. I started having unusual sensations. I felt like shopkeepers, strangers on the streets, and other patrons at the library were looking at me with suspicion like I was hiding something...and I was.

In recalling this situation, I realized this was the first attack of what I came to regard as my "paranoia." Sigmund Freud had given a series of lectures in America about ten years earlier, and since then, people in educated circles talked about his theories. I remembered hearing about paranoia—the fear that people were out to get you. Freud said that sometimes this was caused by a guilty conscience. Recently I sure felt guilty about not getting that divorce before marrying again.

As the clerk processed our marriage license, I shook in my shoes. But, thank God, my marriage to James Savage went undetected!   Like magic, my fearfulness disappeared. Robert and I kissed, and he said, "I can hardly wait to marry you, Baby."

I used my hard-earned money to finally buy a short, modern white dress, white shoes and pearls. As planned, we got married by a Justice of the Peace, and then we went out to celebrate.

We walked hand-in-hand to a place Robert had in mind. He said, "I wish we could go to the Cotton Club. Even though it's in Harlem and has our best entertainers, it's for Whites only."

"Sell-Outs!"

I asked myself, How could Duke Ellington and Ethel Waters go along with that? But maybe it was asking too much of them when they felt driven to entertain and wanted to be paid well for their work— sort of like I felt about my art. I couldn't blame them when I thought about it like that.

Robert said, "I wonder why the Whites want to come down here to clubs in Harlem anyhow."

I thought about that while we walked. "Maybe the Whites want what we have. They see how we let go and have such a good time when we finally have the chance."

My husband turned to me and cracked one of his rare but glorious smiles. "That's probably true, Gussie. Let's let go and kick up our heels!"

And we did.

Within a few months, I became pregnant. Robert was jubilant. He felt it was time for him to be a father. I was less sure. I would have to feed the baby, change its diapers and entertain him or her. Plus, I'd probably still need to do my laundry work. Robert made some, but very little, money in Garvey's Association.

But, despite the fact that our baby would be one more person to add to my busy schedule, he or she would be OUR baby, and that symbol of Robert's and my love would be with us until the day we died.

No matter what, though, I would keep up my artistic career. I finally completed Marcus Garvey's bust. I took a deep breath waiting those few seconds while my subject decided if it looked like him. When he smiled for the first time and said, "You captured me perfectly," I was able to exhale.

He continued, "I am an important man, but not a handsome one. You have duplicated my massive head and small but alert eyes. Most importantly, you have depicted my determination, intelligence, and pride." Garvey was definitely not a humble man.

He paid me the $300 he promised for my work. I had a picture taken of his bust so I could use it to advertise for other commissions. Garvey kept the original in his home and would not let anyone else see it. I wished he would have let me display it in a prominent place...at least for a while. However, he did have small replicas of it created in some factory and sold them to UNIA members.

At about this time, Garvey confided in Robert that the government was giving him problems. The culprit was a young guy named J. Edgar Hoover. Robert explained that Hoover was a special assistant to the Attorney General and head of the General Intelligence Division, also known as "the anti-radical division." Apparently, Hoover was a very suspicious man, and he thought that any individual or group that questioned the U.S. in any way would try to overthrow the entire government. Forget about freedom of speech with him. Robert said Hoover might even view people like me or Langston or

Countee as dangerous because we discussed ways to bring equal rights to all Americans.

Robert was so irate about Hoover spying on Garvey that he could hardly sleep at night. He tossed and turned. I tried to hold him, but I could not anchor him. Only the thought of our baby brought an occasional smile to his face.

Six months into our marriage, Garvey wanted my husband to lead a delegation to Liberia to arrange for mass emigration of American Negroes to that country. Despite my tears and fears, my husband went. Actually, he was thrilled to go. I should have foreseen this, but I had kept ignoring the fact that living in Africa was Garvey and my husband's dream. The group took the ship SS President Grant. When Robert left, he said he would be back in about a month and for me not to worry.

He and two other important people in the UNIA met with the President King of Liberia, but Robert sent me a letter stating they were unable to obtain the permissions and aid they requested. He was furious.

Two weeks later, I heard an unexpected knock at my door. It was Sunday morning. Irene had gone again with her friends to church.

Of course, our landlords were too cheap to install a simple peephole. So, I had to ask, "Who's there?"

"Marcus Garvey," was the answer.

I didn't like hearing his name. Why would he come to my apartment, since he'd never come before?

When I let him in, he said, "Let's sit down for a minute, Augusta."

As we sat together on the couch, fear turned me to stone.

Garvey said, "Robert was bereft, because the king of Liberia refused permission for our American people to come there."

"I know." If that was all, I was happy.

"When Robert got on the ship to come home, he took sick." For the first time ever, Marcus looked rattled. His face crumbled as he said, "It was pneumonia. I am sorry to tell you, Augusta, that he passed away."

"What? No, I don't believe it. There must be some mistake. He was so young and healthy. Maybe they got the wrong person."

Garvey took my limp hand, "I'm sorry, Augusta. Our friends sent a telegram saying it was he who died."

I spoke angrily, "Go, just go. I need to be alone."

Garvey slowly walked to the door as I stayed on the couch. "Goodbye, Augusta. Let me know if you need anything." He left quietly.

I couldn't face it. I lay stomach down on my couch that had been probably used by five families before I got it. I held onto each side of the cushion on my head's side like it was a life raft keeping me afloat. I kept repeating to myself, "No, no, no!"

I tried to hold on until Irene came home. When I heard a key turn the lock, I felt some relief.

Immediately Irene came and stood over me, asking, "What's wrong, Mom?"

"Sit down, I'll tell you."

She sat on the chair opposite of the couch and leaned forward with the most concerned look I'd ever seen on her face.

"It's hard to ex...ex...plain," I said as my teeth chattered on this hot July day. "Marcus says that Robert is...is... dead."

Slowly but surely I repeated what Marcus told me.

Irene kept shaking her head. Seeing as how we were unaccustomed to sharing physical affection—even in the most dire of straights—Irene came as close as she could to comforting me. She walked to the couch and sat on the floor with her back

101

resting on the couch. We were inches away from one another. Dazed like me, she kept repeating over and over again, "It'll be okay, Mom, it'll be okay."

She was probably trying to comfort herself as much as me. My poor daughter loved her new stepfather.

FIFTEEN

I had sustained so many losses. Starting with my little siblings, then going to my beloved husband John, and now this. I was only 33 years old, but I felt like I was 80.

Garvey's group, the United Negro Improvement Association, arranged to give Robert a funeral fit for a king. I avoided the pomp and went down to West Palm Beach to nurse my wounds with my family. Irene had to remain in New York to go to school. I arranged for her to stay with Cynthia across the hall. I had to carry on, because I had Robert's baby in me. He or she would remind me of my dear husband.

Four months later, I gave birth to a healthy baby girl. She was so beautiful—having a pretty brown complexion somewhere between Robert's and my coloring. She looked at me with mahogany eyes that seemed wise beyond that of a newborn. An inkling of hope combated my sorrow. I named my baby Roberta, after my late husband, and I called Irene to tell her the good news. She was eager to meet her baby sister.

We had Roberta sleeping in a bassinet that my mother had made from a basket and to which she attached pretty bows and streamers. Relief washed over me when I found I didn't have the fears I had with Irene. I felt confident feeding, holding and changing Roberta. On the tenth day after she was born, Roberta didn't scream at night to wake me up for a feeding. I woke after a sound sleep and immediately jumped out of bed to check on my baby. I found her motionless.

I held her close to me and patted her back real hard to bring life into her. My mother, father and siblings shrieked and cried. They laid her down on a blanket on the kitchen table and did everything they could—breathing air in and out of her mouth, squeezing her hands and toes. Nothing worked.

"NO!" I screamed.

"No, no, this can't be happening again," I kept repeating.

I looked for whatever I could throw around the house. Screaming all the while, I found a cup and hurtled it against the wall. My older brother grabbed my wrists and looked me in the eyes, "Stop, Gussie!"

I shrieked, "No, I won't. It's not right! Why does God take everyone I love?"

My brother kept holding my wrists. I tried with all my might to pull away. Finally, too weak to stand, I fell to my knees. I cried over and over, "Not again, not again!"

My mother took one of my arms, and my sister took the other. They helped me to the couch. I slipped into my "nothing state" like I did after John died. I just lay there, completely "out of it," trying not to think about anything. I refused food and drink.

Depression took hold of me—pressing on me, holding me down. I knew it wouldn't let me go until it was finished with me. Or maybe it would never let me go. Maybe I had suffered too much to ever be whole again.

Within a week or so, my oldest sister came down from Green Cove Springs. When I first saw her at my side, I noticed threads of gray had woven themselves into her hair and a few wrinkles lined her face, but she still had eyes that said, "I love you, Little Sis, and I'll take care of you." Once again, she slowly and tenderly got me to dress and eat.

But Depression still pressed heavy on me. I said to my sister, "What's the point? Why go on living?"

"How about Irene?"

"At her age, I was married...and so were you. She can take care of herself." I knew I sounded cold, but that's how I felt.

"You're right, Little Sis. But no matter how many loved ones we have or lose we have to keep livin' for ourself."

"And why should I?"

"Why? What do you still want to do with your life?"

I was quiet.

She said, "You know what you want. You want to work with your clay and be a great artist."

I stared at her, thought about it, and then said, "You're right."

It took a couple of months, but eventually I picked myself up and made arrangements to take the train back to New York. It was a sad, lonely ride and when Irene met me at the station, we both choked back tears. I knew my daughter was grieving the loss of the baby sister she never got to meet.

Countee Cullen, Langston Hughes, W.E. B. DuBois, Sadie Peterson and all my other poetry night friends came as a group to comfort me. However, after a few minutes of inquiring about my wellness, they launched into feverish discussions about current events. They didn't just come once. They kept coming. Their conversation helped me temporarily escape from my grief, but, as they rambled on, I sat quietly, retreating into my own little world of mourning.

One evening they were incensed about what was happening to Marcus Garvey. Although none of them favored his "Back to Africa" idea, they were furious that the government was trumping up charges against him. They said J. Edgar Hoover was accusing Garvey of "Mail Fraud." According to Hoover, Garvey had made up and mailed brochures with a picture of a big ship on it that said on its bow, "The Phillis Wheatley." That was the name of a much-heralded Negro poet. Hoover found out that the name on the ship was actually "The Orion," but it had been changed by Garvey who at one time was a printer. From what our group understood, Garvey had actually lined up ships to sail to Liberia and used this ship simply as an example. However, changing its name wasn't too wise because it technically was mail fraud.

From all I heard about him, I hated Hoover. However, I also didn't like hearing anything about Garvey, because his name brought back memories of Robert.

Eventually our group started discussing the theories of a man named Alain Locke. I came out of my shell and commented, "I know you folks mentioned that he first came up with the title the 'New Negro,' but I don't know much else about him."

Langston explained, "He is a Negro philosophy professor at Howard University, although he just got put on some kind of leave of absence for teaching a race relations class that didn't go over well with the administration. I'm surprised you haven't heard more about him. I've had coffee with him a couple of times."

"I imagine he was not a child of slaves." He was probably another lucky one.

"No, he wasn't. His family in Philadelphia was fairly prominent," Countee said.

Sadie stood up, walked to the kitchen and got a glass of water. Coming back into the living room she announced that she wasn't a fan of Locke. "He's kind of like DuBois and Garvey, trying to figure out how we Negroes can gain equality. He's highly educated and has published articles as well as books. I admire him for his efforts, but lately he fashions himself as an art critic. Why, I don't know. He tries to tell Negro artists what to paint or sculpt. For instance, he doesn't like Henry Ossawa Tanner's paintings, because a lot of them depict our people in rural scenes praying, playing the banjo or dancing. And lately

Tanner is painting Christian scenes. He mostly lives in Paris now, and his work is selling. But Alain Locke says he should be dealing with 'African themes' or African art, whatever that means. I'm a librarian, not an artist, but Locke isn't an artist either or an art historian."

Countee also had strong opinions on Locke's theories. "Locke says that our new Negro artists should take cues from Picasso and Modigliani who got excited after they saw African statues and masks taken from Africa and dumped in a Parisian museum's storage area. They were looking for new ideas. So, they started painting abstract pictures of people with flattened faces like African masks.

"Who cares? Let those European guys paint what they wish. Our Negro American artists should have freedom to paint whatever they want without being judged."

This conversation roused me from my doldrums. Everyone looked surprised when I joined in again. "Okay, I learned a little about the African masks and sculpture at Cooper Union. We were told the Africans used an adze—sort of like an axe—to cut into wood. The mouth, nose, eyes and ears looked like they could be of humans or animals. The faces looked flat partly because of the axe they used. They wore the masks for their dances. They used the statues for their own spiritual reasons—not for art. Our culture is different than theirs, Let's admit it. Africans should feel free to create whatever they want for their reasons, and we should feel free to produce whatever we want for our reasons."

Frowning at me, Gwendolyn Bennett said, "But I must say I admire Alain Locke and any academic who is trying to help our race."

I took a long look at Gwendolyn. She was so gifted, although her poetry didn't make much money for her. Like all of us in the poetry group, Gwendolyn had slowly unraveled the story of her life. Her parents got divorced when she was very young and her father kidnapped her. She lived her developing years with her father and stepmother in hiding from her mother. Her dad attended Howard and made sure Gwendolyn went to Howard also.

She also mentioned that she went to an all-White girls' high school. Although Gwendolyn wrote one of their school plays, it must have been challenging for her to fit in. After spending hours with her in our poetry group meetings, I got the impression that Gwendolyn was easily impressed by anyone with high status.

Ignoring Gwendolyn's disapproving look, I kept letting off steam. "And what if artists—like me—who happen to be Colored, want to sculpt or paint something else? For example, what if I sculpted the most beautiful marble bust of a White woman, and it was exhibited with works by other Negro artists, and it was as great as a sculpture by Michelangelo, would Locke still give it a negative review?"

Langston vigorously asserted, "He probably would. Because you're a Negro artist, he'd say you should create something that has to do with Africa."

"Who made him God?" I asked.

To my dismay, Joe Gould discovered that our poetry group often met at my apartment. He showed up a couple of times. Some White people were afraid of coming to Harlem. I wished Joe was. On the two occasions when he came, he monopolized the discussions and kept staring at me. I ignored him.

Group discussion returned to Marcus Garvey, and Countee said Garvey chose to be his own lawyer, a disastrous choice. Garvey spoke for three hours, and his machine gun style was full of venom. This did not sit well with the jurors. In separate trials, two other men who were accused in the same case had lawyers who briefly stated how no harm was meant by the brochures. Those two were let go; Garvey was sentenced to five years in prison.

That was so sad to me. Everyone said Hoover was still behind all this and he believed Garvey was "a communist," intent on taking down our country. I distinctly remember Garvey saying at Madison Square Garden that while some of the communist theories might be advantageous to Negroes, he saw the communists as another bunch of White guys who only wanted their own way. He definitely had no interest in steering his followers towards Communism.

We lamented about how Hoover "had it out" for Garvey.

Langston Hughes said, "What will happen if we speak up for racial equality and against things like lynching and Jim Crow laws? Will Hoover go after us?" He was silent for a moment, and then said, "I, for one, will not be silenced."

We all agreed, but quietly. No one looked forward to being destroyed by J. Edgar Hoover.

Joe Gould began writing me letters. I heard through the grapevine that he said we were having an affair. I did not want to give him the satisfaction of responding to his letters or what I heard, but my anger rose almost to the level of a savage heart explosion.

One evening when we were having a poetry group discussion, I heard someone knock and then open the door. I left the door slightly ajar for the meetings, since I didn't feel like running to the door every time someone arrived. I would never repeat that mistake. There at the door was Joe Gould, smiling from ear to ear.

I yelled, "Get out of here, Joe Gould, and never set foot in here again!"

Joe took a step forward anyhow. Countee and Langston rose, stood next to him, and stared him down.

"You must leave...now!" Countee said, loud and clear. "We know how you've been talking behind Augusta's back and sending her those letters."

Joe tried to defend himself, "But I know Augusta cares about me. She's just ashamed of acknowledging it because I'm White and she's embarrassed..."

At that, I stood up and did something I had never done before. I pulled my arm back and tried to punch Joe in the nose. Two of the men held me back.

Countee and Langston tried to push Joe out. He resisted. Joe grunted and yelled, but the men finally shoved him out, locked the door, and attached the chain.

Joe yelled through the door, "You haven't heard the last from me!"

I fumed. Gwendolyn had me sit down and try to compose myself. I feared I would never be free of Joe Gould.

SIXTEEN

From then on, I always used the chain on my door. However, I did occasionally fear that Joe would jump out at me from nowhere as I walked down the street.

But I was still most angry about losing Robert and Roberta, not to mention John. When Irene wasn't home, I thought of all my lost loved ones. I went back to yelling at God, "Why? Why me, God? Why have you seen fit to punish me so often?" Sometimes my anger reverted to Depression. It was hard for me to go to my laundry job.

What finally helped me get free from Depression's hold was remembering what my sister said, "You've got yourself, Gussie. That's all any of us have when it comes right down to it—ourself."
And then I thought of the words of a mother to her child in Langston Hughes' poem,

> So, boy, don't you turn back.
> Don't you set down on the steps
> "Cause you finds it kinder hard.
> Don't you fall now___
> For I'se still goin', honey,
> I'se still climbin',
> And life for me ain't been no crystal stair.

I decided to go on. And the way I would do it would be to take care of myself and do what I loved best, independent of anyone else. I would have to work at the laundry, but I would spend every other hour on my sculpture.

I began molding my clay again.

When Langston, Sadie, Gwendolyn, Countee and W.E.B. came over, they asked to look into my

111

bedroom/studio to see my latest creations. "My God, you've got talent," DuBois said.

On one of his visits, DuBois surprised me. He said he had quietly gone behind the scenes and arranged a scholarship for me to the Royal Academy of Fine Arts in Rome. He was so excited you would think he was getting the scholarship. "This will be perfect for you! It provides tuition and working materials."

I laughed off-handedly. "Yeah, but where am I going to get all the money needed for transportation and living expenses?"

Countee said, "We can raise the money for you...maybe."

"Nobody's going to donate after they gave so I could go to Fontainebleau, which fell apart," I said.

Everyone shook their heads in sad agreement.

I told DuBois I appreciated all his efforts, but it wasn't my time.

After this, DuBois wrote an article for the NAACP's magazine *Crisis,* saying *"There is tonight a Black woman molding clay by herself in a little dark room. Surely, there are doors she might burst through, but when God makes a sculptor, he does not make the pushing sort of person who beats through doors thrust in his face."*

SEVENTEEN

One September evening as Irene and I listened to the radio, we heard that a powerful hurricane threatened Florida. It left a path of devastation in Puerto Rico and some islands I'd never heard of. The reporter said it was barreling towards Palm Beach with winds of 145mph. He said problems could be the worst around Lake Okeechobee, where two of my brothers lived. The water could pour out of the lake and cause serious flooding.

A few minutes later my brother called me from the house where he lived with his wife, nephew and my other brother. His voice shook. "I'm scared, Gussie. The water is coming at us like crazy. It keeps risin' and risin'!"

"Everything will be all right." I tried to reassure him, hoping the fear I was actually feeling wouldn't come through in my voice.

Then I heard the gurgling of water and a long buzzing sound. My brother must have lost hold of the phone.

Irene and I stayed up all night praying and pacing. The phone lines didn't work when we tried to call back. A day later my sister-in-law called, crying. She said they had to sit on their roof because the water got so high. As they waited for help, a surge of water knocked them down. They fell into the rushing water. The current pulled them at breakneck speed, but they were able to grab onto trees. My brother reached out to help a man caught up by the current, but my brother lost his own grip. His body hurtled forward. My other family members clung to their trees—shivering and crying—until the morning when the winds stopped and the water levels went down. People came and picked them up in boats. They found my brother's lifeless body rammed into the back of a wagon that got tangled up with a tree. We heard on the radio later that this massive storm, dubbed The Okeechobee Hurricane, killed over 4,000 people.

My brother was so brave to try to save someone else, but we were all terribly shaken. I cried to myself, *When will I ever quit losing my loved ones—especially in such tragic ways*? But remembering my older sister's words and Langston's poem, I tried not to dwell on my sorrow too much. Plus, I had work to do. I had to help my brother's grief-stricken wife and the rest of my family. The Red Cross was sending my other brother, sister-in-law, and nephew to come stay with us.

When the three of them arrived in New York City, they were amazed at the skyscrapers and crowds. They didn't like the big city, but they were determined to get themselves on their feet. They slept on the couch and on quilts on the floor. While my sister-in-law cried, my brother looked for a job. He was not afraid of hard work. My nephew, Ellis, lay on the couch all day.

Irene tried to draw him out, "I bet it was terrible going through what you did."

Ellis spoke only briefly. "It was. The worst part was Uncle dying." Ellis had wrinkles for a young guy. I knew suffering could do that to you. The only thing he did was to occasionally go outside—always wearing his jaunty cap.

Within a couple of months, my family members got their own apartment a few blocks from where we lived. Irene and I wished them well. My daughter said, "It was good that we helped, but I'm glad to get my privacy back."

I agreed. Although I felt guilty about trying to move on so quickly, I was determined to pursue my own happiness.

I looked for subjects to sculpt. My passion was still to sculpt the heads of my Negro brothers and sisters. In all the art history books I studied at the library, I saw no other busts of my people.

EIGHTEEN

On an especially hot day I sat outside on our front stairs, smoking. I took up this nasty habit to settle my nerves, although I don't think it really helped.

When I began smoking, Irene reprimanded me, "Smoke outside, I hate that smell."

So, I'd go outside. Sitting there on the steps, I watched the children skip rope, play pick-up sticks, and roll dice. I got sad thinking about what Roberta might have been like if she were to become their age.

As I brooded, I saw a boy walking down the street, a boy who seemed alone …almost lost. I had seen him before when I sat outside. His knickers were dirty, and his stockings were torn. He wore a cap pushed to the side. He walked slowly like he had nowhere to go, but he had a swagger.

"Hi there," I said.

He looked around like he didn't think I was talking to him.

I said nicely but firmly, "You, that's right. I'm talking to you."

He frowned. "Yeah, what do you want?"

I stood up and stepped on my cigarette. I extended my hand. "I'm Augusta Savage. I make people's pictures out of clay. You have an interesting face. Maybe I could sculpt you?"

The boy looked puzzled. Eventually he said, "What's in it for me?"

"You come up to my place where my daughter also lives, and you sit and pose for me…a few times. I'll give you food and any pocket change I have."

He stared at me.

I said, "Perhaps you have parents. Perhaps you think they may not like this. I could ask their permission…"

The boy waved me off. "No parents. I'll do it. Do you happen to have any food now?"

I asked his name, took him up to my apartment and introduced him to my daughter.

"Irene, David is going to pose for a new piece. He'll be coming over once in a while."

Irene sighed with obvious displeasure.

I got out some greens and cornbread for David. I motioned for him to sit on a chair at our kitchen table. The way the chair wobbled when he sat down shook his cool demeanor for a moment. After he ate, I got out my clay and had him pose. David looked to be about thirteen years old. His lopsided grin made him look impish, but his half-closed eyes appeared world-weary. This was the unlikely combination I wanted to capture.

Over the course of his sittings, I enjoyed getting to know David. I asked him about his life, and he told me stories of things he did, like searching through dumpsters for food and sneaking onto trolleys without paying. David told me about his friends— other boys who, like him, strode through the world without parents. They made small fires at night to keep warm, smoked discarded cigarette butts, and shared stories of their adventures. I came to admire this spunky kid.

When I was three quarters of the way finished with his bust, David quit coming. Two more weeks passed, and no sign of David. I walked around the neighborhood, searching. But still, no David.

I feared that something bad happened to him, and, quite selfishly, I worried that I wouldn't be able to finish his bust adequately. After pondering the situation for some time, I came up with a solution. Since my nephew Ellis had some of David's looks and attitude, perhaps he would pose. I'd offer him the same meager payment as I did David. I couldn't afford any more.

Still sullen, but eager to accept free meals and pocket change, Ellis agreed. After a few sittings and my completion of the piece, Irene commented on how it looked like both Ellis and David.

Irene surprised me by complimenting my work. "I love the way you captured the wrinkles in his shirt and the way his cap lays."

*****

Whenever the usual crowd came over, I cleaned my bedroom/studio, because, as usual, someone would peek inside to see my latest project. This time it was Langston who looked in. He called, "Come here everyone, and look at this!"

Immediately, they got up and crooned over my David/Ellis bust. Gwendolyn Bennett said in a snide manner, "He looks like a street urchin."

I gave her a dirty look. "So?"

She stuttered, "I didn't…I didn't mean to be critical."

Even if she exuded an air of superiority, Gwendolyn was one of the few women in our group, so I wanted to remain her friend. I forced a smile. "That's okay, Gwendolyn."

Undeterred, I told everyone how I discovered David and came to admire him and about how Ellis helped me finish off the piece.

Langston said, "Perhaps you should title this sculpture, '*Gamin.*' It's a fancy word for street kid."

I did just that.

The group encouraged me to let the 135th St. Library display my *Gamin* sculpture. Word got around that it was special. Eugene Kinckle Jones of the National Urban League came to see it along with John E. Nail, a real estate operator and brother-in-law of James Weldon Johnson. James had come to a couple of our library group meetings. He said he had

118

told Jones and Nail about my talent, and he'd suggested they go to view my *Gamin*.

"Maybe they can help you in some way," James said. "It takes money and backing to make it in the arts." I couldn't have agreed more.

In the meantime, something else commanded my attention. On a cold, snowy evening, I heard a loud ringing. I was lying under a quilt in the front room listening to the radio. I still couldn't get used to the new-fangled machine called a telephone. It rang so loudly and interrupted me usually at moments when I felt most at peace. Of course, Irene always expected it was a friend calling. She bolted from her room and picked up the receiver.

Her voice shook, and she grimaced. "Oh no, really?"

I joined her at the phone. "What happened?"

"Here you talk to Grandma," and Irene handed me the phone.

My father had a stroke. My mother told me that half of his body, including his mouth, was paralyzed. My parents had no one to help them because my brothers and sisters had moved from West Palm Beach to other towns with better jobs.

"What should we do, Gussie?" Mama cried.

"Let me think about it. I'll get back to you," I answered. "And give Daddy my love."

It only took me a day to decide what to do. Irene was an influence. "Mom, we have to bring them up here. Grandpa's in really bad shape, and you know Grandma is old and can hardly walk any more. I'll help you with them. You know how much I love Grandma and Grandpa."

NINETEEN

And so I decided my mother and father could come live with us. My decision was not without sacrifice. I would have to give up my bedroom/studio. The sofa with the sunken-down cushions would be my bed.

Langston's poem ran through my mind, "Life ain't been no crystal stair."

While my parents were planning their trip up north, my thoughts went back to how those two big businessmen, Nail and Jones, who had gone to see *Gamin*. Hoping they were impressed, I was thankful that James Weldon Johnson had mentioned my sculpture to them.

After our poetry group meetings, James and I got to know each other better. We both came from northern Florida. He was a teacher near Jacksonville when I attended school in Green Cove Springs. His great love was writing poetry and especially song lyrics. He wrote a song called "Lift Every Voice and Sing" that we sang at school after we said the Pledge of Allegiance. The song was like our Negro National Anthem.

Over the course of our group meetings, James revealed different aspects of his life. Besides writing music, James wanted to help our people, and so he became secretary of the NAACP. In 1915, he traveled to Haiti to investigate conditions there. He talked about how Haiti was occupied by our Marines, supposedly because of political unrest. Five years later he wrote a series of articles in *The Nation* in which he described the American occupation as brutal. He had roots in Haiti. His great grandparents had left Haiti after the revolutionary upheaval in 1802.

Like many of our other group members, James had a university degree. His parents were not children of slaves. James spoke with the sophistication of The Talented Tenth. Yet, he was so nice and respectful to me and everyone else that I felt like an equal with him.

Occasionally, I felt inferior with our other group members, who were born into a higher class. Even though everyone was happy to come and discuss things at my dumpy apartment, they sometimes looked right past me when they discussed complicated political issues.

The men always wore suits. I thought this indicated they were wealthy. But, looking back, I have to admit their clothes looked a little threadbare. Perhaps they didn't have much more money than me.

I always dressed simply but nicely. I kept a slim figure and rotated among three or four form-fitting dresses that I bought at a resale shop. I pulled my hair back neatly unless I was going out on the town. In regards to the other ladies in the group, Gwendolyn Bennett often looked like she cared less about her appearance, but when there was a big affair at the library, she dressed elegantly, wore a sophisticated hat, and lipstick with ample makeup. You would never know she was the same person.

Zora Neale Hurston attended our group infrequently, but when she did, her presence was overwhelming. One time she strode into the room and flung a long, colorful scarf around her neck, bellowing out the title of her latest book. She knew how to promote her work and to make an entrance, but in the kitchen she whispered to me that no matter how much acclaim she received, she didn't reap much money from her book sales.

I finally learned that Mr. Nail and Mr. Jones were so impressed with my *Gamin* sculpture that they approached the Julius Rosenwald Fund established by the president of Sears Roebuck to help minority groups. An expert was assigned to evaluate my work. When she saw *Gamin*, she liked it so much that she recommended the Fund award me two successive fellowships to study in Europe. Usually, $1,500 was granted, but they would give me $1,800 per year, because I had serious financial need. I couldn't believe it! I would take this offer. My time had come!

This was a whole six years after my Fontainebleau experience. I was amazed at the outpouring of support. Although the Rosenwald Fund took care of all the basics, people assumed I could use additional money for clothes and miscellaneous needs. Fund-raising activities were held in Harlem and Greenwich Village. Negro women's groups sent money. Negro professors at Florida A and M where I had attended school for a year sent $50. W.E. B. DuBois sent a letter of introduction about me to Elisabeth Prophet, a renowned American sculptor in Paris, asking her to help me get situated in my new surroundings.

I called James Weldon Johnson to thank him profusely for recommending my work to Nail and Jones and to tell him about how people were donating money for my expenses. I didn't have to see his face to know he was beaming with admiration when he said, "You are a true artist of the people, Gussie. Your supporters have known the pain of discrimination and poverty and want to help someone like them with talent to succeed."

I felt like I'd climbed almost all the way up the stairway to success. I was so full of hope and enthusiasm I could hardly sleep at night. I chose to use the scholarship to study in France. I imagined that if I could improve upon my talents in France, I could create a variety of sculptures in the U.S.—not just busts—that would actually sell. Maybe I could even afford my own studio, get a nice apartment, and quit my lousy laundry job.

There still remained the challenge of my parents. My one brother who stayed in West Palm Beach put them on a train to New York. No easy task. When Irene and I set eyes on them at the station, I was shocked by what I saw. My father was in a wheelchair; my hobbled mother could barely push it. She had aged so much in the last couple of years! When I exchanged glances with Irene, she too had dismay written on her face.

My mother looked like she might have a stroke herself as she viewed the station's frantic hubbub. On the other hand, the new sights made my father's eyes open wider than they'd been probably since he had his stroke.

Prior to their coming, I had a talk with Irene. "I'm sorry, Baby, but you're going to have to take care of your grandparents for a while. You know I just got this scholarship to study in France."

Her shoulders sagged, but her tone was brave. "I know. I'm out of school now. I'll get some extra hours at the laundry, and I'll take care of them."

"Remember, your aunts and uncles will chip in and give $20 a month to help with the expenses, and I'll send any money I can."

As much as she loved her grandparents, I could see that this was not the way Irene wanted to live her life as a young adult. I asked myself, *What kind of mother am I to leave her behind to deal with all this?*

Regardless of my guilt, I stuck with my decision to leave. Before my departure, I heard a knock. I opened the door only the few inches that the chain permitted. It was Joe Gould! Before I could slam the door on him, he threw a folded note into the opening and, without saying a word, he ran down the stairs. The note simply said, "Will you marry me?" I crumbled it and threw it in the garbage. "Hell, no!" I yelled to the air.

123

My chance to study in Paris came just at the right time. I could blot Joe Gould out of my mind. After all, I'd soon be thousands of miles away.

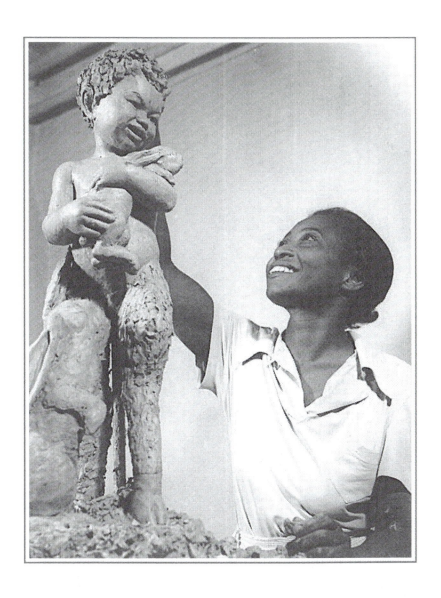

Augusta with her Creation

(WPA)

Gamin

Smithsonian American Art Museum,
gift of Benjamin and Olya Margolin

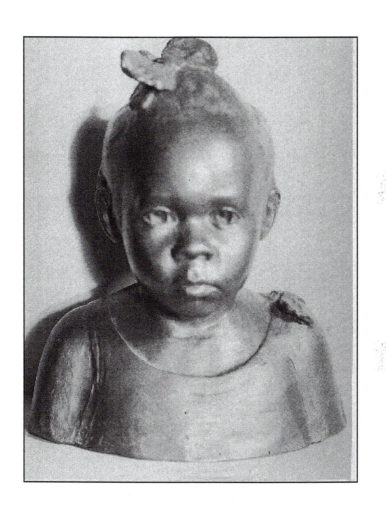

Lenore

Augusta Savage at Work

WPA

Realization

Image from the Smithsonian American Art Museum

Augusta Savage sculpting her

"Lift Every Voice and Sing"

sculpture

The Harp

The Harp Sculpture at the 1939
New York World's Fair
NYPL Digital Collections

Part Three

TWENTY

Boarding the ocean liner to France, I was nervous. Perhaps there would be high waves and storms the ship couldn't handle. The wealthier people with expensive tickets could afford the best accommodations, but I didn't mind staying in the meager quarters. I figured anything would be better than traveling with those Fontainebleau girls, who would have felt so "uncomfortable" with me.

Within a couple of days, I found our big ship could handle anything. I relaxed. The sky and the water blended together as one. The hint of salt water in my mouth and the feel of the ocean breeze reminded me of Palm Beach. After about ten days, we went through the English Channel and docked at La Havre, France.

I got on a train and made it in three hours to Paris. Having found my way around New York City just eight years earlier, I was not so intimidated by a new city. Actually, I felt thrilled when I arrived in Paris. Starting from my humble beginnings in Green Cove Springs, I was amazed at how far I had come.

In Paris, the man at the railroad information desk gave me directions to the Acadèmie de la Grande Chaumière, where I wanted to find someone to instruct me privately. I paid for a temporary, tiny room near the school in the fifth arrondissement at 50, Rue des Ecoles (the Parisian addresses sounded so fancy). I called Elizabeth Prophet, the American to whom Dubois had referred me.

"Bonjour," she said, but her voice was flat, like she'd just woken up even though it was early afternoon.

I gushed, "Oh, *bonjour* back. It's me—Augusta Savage—from America. I believe Dubois told you about me."

"Sorry, I'm busy," she growled. "I'll get back to you later." She plunked down the phone. I had heard Elizabeth could be crabby.

However, a couple of days later she dropped in and told me she wanted to be of help. She was a slender (almost gaunt-looking) woman with delicate, pretty features. She told me her mother was Negro and her father was Narragansett Indian.

Her callused hands gave witness to her work as a stone and marble sculptor. All she talked about was her sculpting. Elizabeth seemed so serious and so dreary. It made me think, *Even though I am a serious artist, I hope I remain capable of smiling and having fun.* Regardless, it was nice to meet someone from back home with whom I could speak English.

Thankfully, Elizabeth helped me get a better apartment on a tiny street at 3 Impasse de l'Astrolabe near the intersection of the Rue de Vaugirard and the Boulevard du Montparnasse (another mouthful of fancy French words). The neighborhood was a haven for art students. On the sidewalks and in the parks, I saw people painting and drawing on big easels.

Elizabeth said, "You have probably heard about Montmartre where Monet, Renoir and other artists worked in the generation before us. Montparnasse is the new Montmartre. You may see Modigliani, Picasso or Brancusi walking about. Ernest Hemingway and his writer friends strike up fervent discussions at our coffee shops."

How exciting, I thought.

My little studio apartment in Montparnasse didn't have heat, but it did have rats. The other artists lived in the same conditions. Yet, you could almost touch the strong presence of hope and excitement in the air. Young artists displayed their paintings next to their easels and sold them for almost nothing. I wondered how many of these works would someday be expensive collectors' items. At least half of them included people's faces in distorted variations of African masks; Alain Locke would have loved them.

There were other Negroes in the neighborhood—artists, writers and musicians. Sometimes we chatted in passing or sat down on a bench and talked. When we introduced ourselves, people recognized my name. I had become a celebrity! Unfortunately, this was mostly due to the Fontainebleau fiasco.

Most of my new acquaintances were from the States but not all from New York City. They asked about Harlem and raved about our jazz.

I was pretty much on my own to decide how to spend my grant money. Writing to Countee across the miles, I said, "This is exciting but frightening."

When I inquired at the Acàdemie as to who might be teaching sculpture to independent students, they gave me the name and address of Fèlix Benneteau-Desgrois, I walked about six blocks to his studio. Like most artists, he kept his door open and his windows unshuttered so potential buyers could come in.

When I set eyes on Monsieur Benneteau-Desgrois, I thought, *This is one handsome man.* He looked very sophisticated—how I imagined a typical, refined Parisian would. His short black hair was cut in the latest style; his vested suit was perfectly tailored to fit his slender frame; and his dark brown eyes were friendly, but intense at the same time.

"*Bonjour,*" I said in what was probably a sheepish voice, not knowing if we could communicate beyond a simple hello.

135

"*Bonjour*," he replied, as he turned from a bust he was sculpting. Very pleasantly, he asked me something in French.

I used a phrase I knew would come in handy. "*Je ne parle pas francais*," meaning "I don't speak French."

He still looked at me with an encouraging smile.

I went over to one of his busts sitting on a pedestal. Looking at him for permission, I touched it. Then I took out a picture of my *Gamin* sculpture and said in English, "I want to learn from you."

He understood better when I asked in one of my other French words, "*Professeur...* (teacher*)?*"

Ever so politely, he asked, "*Argent?*"

I raised my hands and gave him a perplexed look.

Still smiling, he dug into his pocket and pulled out some French coins. "*Argent,*" he said again.

Eagerly, I shook my head, "Yes, Yes. Or *Oui, oui*. I will give you *argent*."

The rest became history. He took me on as a student. Many of his busts were of famous Parisian politicians and entertainers. He had me sit with him as he worked, and he taught me techniques about how to sculpt a subject's torso and clothing as well as his or her head. He sculpted most of his subjects from the waist up.

Every afternoon I pored over a book of French words and their translations, and I practiced the words with my *professeur.* He spoke very slowly to me, and within a few weeks I started mastering basic French.

One day, he said, "There is a competition for a medallion to be used for the upcoming Paris Colonial Exhibition."

Seeing that he lost me, he got out a book from Paris' last colonial exhibition and showed me

136

pictures, including a medallion. He used the word *"argent"* again to explain that I could win prize money for designing a medallion for the exhibition. Of course, I took on the challenge, and I won the contest. I wished my mother could be here to witness my success. However, I hated the idea of the exposition bragging about how great Paris was for colonizing other countries.

Strict, but patient, my *professeur* also promised to enter my work in a Paris Salon Exhibition, if I worked hard. And, much to my joy, I won citations—not ribbons, but at least citations—at the fall and spring Salons.

Eventually, I felt I had learned all I could from this talented sculptor. I had to find someone else who could teach me more. On my last day with Monsieur Benneteau-Desgrois, it was hard to leave. As we pressed each other in a goodbye embrace, the feel of his wool jacket and the smell of his hair pomade made me wish we could be more than student-teacher. However, I knew it was best this way, and he hadn't really hinted at it being more.

Inquiring again at the Acadèmie, I found out about Charles Despiau, a sculptor who supposedly put his own distinctive twist on the classical style. His storefront studio was much like Benneteau's. When I met him, I felt I was looking at a version of Joe Gould. Despiau was a short, thin man, who wore a rumpled tweed suit and a hat like the reporters back in New York City. In one hand he held a sculpting tool and in another a cigarette. I almost expected him to pull out a notebook and start asking questions like Joe did.

But, thankfully, Despiau was a lot different than Joe. Although he was friendly, he was a hard worker, and, when he sculpted, he became very quiet. Despiau spoke some English, and my French was improving. So, communication was easier with him than with Benneteau.

137

He explained, "I work in what I call the 'archaic classical' style. For inspiration, I draw upon 'archaic' sculptures—namely the first sculptures of the Greeks—to make simple sculptures of parts of the human body, sometimes just a man's torso and half of his arms but not his head." I remembered studying ancient Greek sculpture at the 135th St. library and seeing how only a part of a sculpture remained while the rest was broken off over the annals of time.

I thought I might as well try working with him. I needed to expand my skills beyond that of sculpting busts. He instructed me to make small-scale clay depictions of people standing, sitting, or caught in an odd position. Then he critiqued my creations.

One day Despiau said, "Your education would be greatly enhanced if you traveled to find examples of archaic sculptures in Europe's oldest cathedrals and churches."

Who could pass up such advice from one's art teacher? I requested the Rosenwald Fund to send me two fellowship installments at one time so I could tour Europe's historic buildings. In my heart, I thanked Mr. Johnson, my teacher back in Green Cove Springs, who schooled me so well in English that I could write such a proposal. However, the Rosenwald Fund was unwilling. *Oh well, nice try,* I thought. But then I tried the Carnegie Corporation. Much to my delight, they came through and sent me the money I needed.

And, so, I took trains to Belgium, Germany, and various parts of France. For about three weeks, I observed the sculpture that decorated church portals and interiors. How I loved those travels! Aside from viewing the art, I enjoyed hearing the languages and tasting the foods from different countries. Also, I liked that in Europe I could stay wherever I chose, eat wherever I wanted, and ride in whatever railcar I desired. My race was not a problem.

Although I studied archaic sculpture in the oldest of the churches, I preferred the more detailed, humanistic, sculpture of the Renaissance. On my visit to Italy, I fell in love with Michelangelo's paintings in the Sistine Chapel ceiling and his sculpture of David. His subjects looked so full of muscle, heart and soul.

When I returned to Montparnasse, I was still very inspired by the classical and Renaissance sculpture I had observed, but I decided to try out new things. I thought, *I will do this now while I am a student and no one is judging me.* I experimented with the concept that everything could be a subject—a bird, a feather, anything—and it was fun sculpting those things.

Six months after designing my medallion for the Paris Colonial Exhibition, I actually attended the event. Exposition signs talked about how Paris and other countries (including the U.S.) supposedly helped their colonies: the colonizer benefited from the resources of their colonies, but in turn (supposedly) the inhabitants progressed from their savage state to becoming civilized. Savage: that word hit me hard, partly because of my last name and partly because I thought of my heart as savage when I flew into rages. I tried to reassure myself, *I've only done that in a few extreme situations.*

In the Dahomean exhibit, a few families from Africa, were standing outside a "traditional hut," although it was designed by the French. The newspapers said the entertainers were paid in their countries' currencies, but the frowns of the Dahomeans bore witness to the fact that they probably regretted taking the money and coming to Paris. Spectators acted like they were peering at animals in a zoo. Because the Dahomean women were bare-breasted, the European children pointed to them and giggled. When the women began dancing, they looked like they were trying to replicate their tribal dance, but their movements were awkward, as the spectators leered. Personally, I greatly admired the way the women looked. Most were tall and muscular, although the setting took away from their dignity and power.

I went to a library in Paris that afternoon to do some research. I read that until about a hundred years earlier Dahomean kings had female warriors who defended the palace.

The next day I went back to the Dahomean exhibition. Using my basic French, I wanted to pull one of the women to the side and talk with her. I imagined she would speak some French also, since her country was overrun with French soldiers and merchants.

Luckily, a woman did respond to me as I smiled and bowed slightly to communicate my respect.

In French, I introduced myself, "I am Augusta Savage. I am an artist, and I admire you and your people."

She smiled back but in a tentative way. After studying me for a few seconds, she said, "I am pleased to meet you. I am Falhome."

"I am actually a sculptor. I make statues of people."

Falhome responded, "We have people in our land who make statues, too."

"I have a request of you, Falhome, and you are welcome to refuse it, if you wish. However, I would like to make a statue of you, because you look so magnificent, strong and powerful. I want people to recognize these qualities of the Dahomean women. I will pay you something in French money, since that's the only kind I have."

She stood a little straighter and said "Yes, I will do that, but only if you show me in a way that truly honors my people. No money will be needed then."

"I would like to do that," I said in a reverent tone.

So, I had Falhome come to my place on some of her days off. Following Monsieur Benneteau's example, I created two life-size clay sculptures of her from the waist up although, in this case, she was unclothed. I showed Falhome looking up and to the left, seeming to listen for something important. In the other, I posed her looking up fiercely and carrying a spear, perhaps readying herself for battle. In both, I portrayed her as a strong, intelligent Negro woman.

When she examined the two completed statues, she smiled broadly. "Yes, this is the way I want the women of Dahomey to be known."

Falhome absolutely would not accept any money. I thanked her profusely and gave her a sculpture of a duck that I molded just for her. She giggled when she received it. I don't know if ducks inhabited her part of the world.

I knew that Alain Locke would approve of these statues of Falhome because they were so "African," but I did them just because I wanted to. Not because he said I should.

I believe I was the first person in the United States to sculpt a partially nude female Negro. That made me proud. Before Falhome left, she asked, "Can I bring my family to see these?"

"Oh, yes," I said eagerly, "but you can see there is not much room here."

The next day she knocked on my door, and I looked out to see about fifteen people standing with her. I welcomed them and ushered in five or so at a time for a viewing. In the last group was a boy of about sixteen. He had noticeable muscles and beautiful facial features. I asked Falhome if that was her son; he looked just like her. When she said "yes," I asked her and him if he could pose for me.

"Would you like her to make a statue of you, Jean?" Falhome asked her son.

141

In a quiet, humble way, he answered, "Yes."

"That is good, Jean. I know you will bring more glory to our Dahomean people," Falhome said.

So, I did an almost life-size statue of Jean on his knees but leaning forward as he looked out into the distance. It was a challenging piece, seeing as how I put the boy's body in such a unique position. This was when I appreciated how Monsieur Desgrois taught me to sculpt people in all different positions. The boy was in his natural state with only a small piece of cloth covering him. I named that sculpture The Call. Another work that Locke would have liked.

Countee Cullen sent me a letter. He said he received a Guggenheim award to study in Paris. A couple of weeks later when he arrived, I gave him a big hug—rare for me, but I really liked this man. As usual, Countee got the social ball rolling. He introduced me to the noted Negro American painter, Henry Ossawa Tanner, whom we had discussed back home shortly before I left. I met Countee at cafés and bistros where the conversation often turned to how we Negroes could be ourselves in Paris…more so than in the United States.

On one rainy spring day, Countee and the rest of our gang sat inside a bistro and treated ourselves to a rare restaurant meal. In walked a White gentleman who shivered as he took down his umbrella and put it in a stand near the door. As the waiter walked him to a table, the man looked at our group. He immediately recognized Countee. My friend stood up and shook the man's hand. He said this was the famous poet and writer from back home, e.e.Cummings. He invited e.e. to sit with us. Immediately, I was aware that e.e. was staring at me in particular.

"I bet you're Augusta Savage," he said.

With a hint of flirtation, I asked, "And how would you know?"

"Someone from back in the States asked me to look for 'a young woman with almond eyes, a delicate elegance and an extraordinarily soft voice.' Those were his exact words."

A pang of fear seized my heart.

e.e. took a note out of his pocket and said, "Joe Gould asked me to give this to you if I saw you in Paris."

I took the note without reading it, and crumbled it with a furious expression that probably frightened e.e..

Countee said, "Joe Gould has been stalking Augusta. She has always made it clear that she wants nothing to do with him."

I put my head into my hands that by now were trembling.

e.e. said, "I'm so, so sorry, Miss Savage. I had no idea he was bothering you. I once saw potential in Joe as a writer, but he is a troubled—and now I find—cruel man."

It took me a while to recover. I finally said, "I thought I was free of him because I am an ocean away from America." I sighed, then suggested, "Let's change the subject."

So, e.e. started talking about something he called The Depression and said that people back home were suffering from it. Since I received the same amount of grant money every month, I paid little attention to economics. Having heard from despicable Joe again, my mind was in a fog for the rest of the evening anyhow.

In my next letter, I asked Irene if she and my parents were affected by this thing called The Depression. Irene didn't mention it in her return letter.

TWENTY-ONE

I had heard about Josephine Baker back in the United States when she performed in a hit musical with lots of dancing called "Shuffle Along." In Paris, I saw posters about her starring at a club on one of the most famous boulevards in the world—the Champs-Élysées. I rarely went to that part of Paris. Everything about it was too expensive for my pocketbook. However, on this occasion I decided to splurge. It was so rare to find a famous, female Negro artist. And so, I went out "on the town" wearing the dress from my wedding to Robert.

The audience was full of White men and women with only a handful of Negroes. After opening acts like juggling and puppetry, Josephine made her grand entrance. She wore heavy makeup and had her short hair slicked down. In a scanty outfit, she began dancing with unbounded energy. People clapped and cheered. A large band accompanied her. Josephine did wild Charleston moves and made funny facial expressions like crossing her eyes and winking. Everyone roared with enjoyment.

Perhaps that was why this era—back in America as well as in Paris— earned the title of *The Roaring Twenties*. After about an hour, Josephine went backstage and reappeared donning a more sophisticated flapper dress with, of all things, a leopard. We all shrieked with fear. Josephine walked him around with a leash and then returned him backstage. Then she did a dance that was different from her first one. It was slinky, sophisticated, and provocative. The audience received this version of Josephine as enthusiastically as her unbounded energy style.

Josephine exuded great confidence in her body, and that was something I envied her for. I wanted to meet her, and, so I summoned the courage to go backstage. The manager said I could have a word with her before she entered her dressing room.

Still breathless from her vigorous dancing, Josephine gave me a welcoming smile and said, "Hello. I noticed you out there—one of the few Negro women."

"Hello to you. I'm Augusta Savage, a sculptor from the States. I just had to congratulate you on your performance."

Looking puzzled, Josephine said, "Augusta Savage...a sculptor...that name rings a bell. I've heard of you." She paused for a moment, seeming to search her memory. "The Fontainebleau thing. I was still in the States when that happened. Ridiculous, what they did to you!"

"That's for sure."

"You know Miss Savage..."

"Call me Gussie."

"All right. And you call me Josephine. Anyhow, I left the U.S. because of that kind of stuff. And I refused to perform when only Whites were allowed—like at The Cotton Club. We Negroes do all the entertainin', and the management will only let Whites in. What nonsense! We have to let people know we ain't their puppets on a string."

I nodded my head in agreement.

It seemed like Josephine was looking me over, as if sizing up what kind of person I was. She must have approved, because she said, "I got to change now. You can see I'm all hot and sweaty, and I'm goin' out some more tonight. I'll tell you what, Gussie, why don't we meet at that little café on the corner Monday morning at ten and talk some more?"

Walking home that evening, I thought about how I admired Josephine for her convictions as well as her performance. However, I wondered about the audience's reactions. Did they see her as a wild, primitive being that stimulated their sexual fantasies? Or did they just enjoy the feeling of "letting go" in wild abandonment like she did? Or a combination of both? Something bothered me about the show, but I was not an expert on music, dance or sociology. Let someone else figure all that out.

On the Monday of our meeting, I was very excited to talk with Josephine again. When I stepped outside, a perfect spring day greeted me. Vendors sold sweet-smelling flowers, birds sang (with French accents, of course), and couples held hands. It felt good to be alive. The only thing that I wished for was Robert to be here, in person, not just in my heart.

As I walked along, I gave silent thanks, as I often did, to the laundresses, teachers, bakers, and other working people back home who chipped in to pay for my personal expenses. Also, I wafted a prayer of thanks to the heavens above for the Rosenwald and Carnegie Foundations.

To get to the cafè, I had to take my favorite journey in Paris— through the Jardin di Luxembourg, across the Pont Noir Bridge, and past The Notre Dame Cathedral.

I loved the garden and the bridge, but Notre Dame always stole my heart more than any place in Paris. I could gaze at the cathedral a hundred times and still see something new. The stately building imposed itself with a dignity and strength that proclaimed, "I am the centerpiece of Paris." As a sculptor, my favorite part was the three portals on the massive doors leading into the church. Bible heroes adorned each portal. They looked like they were alive and gazing right at me. That was my kind of sculpture!

Everything in Paris was Old World, and beautifully so. The buildings were crowded right next to each other, but each facade was different. Some had columns built into the walls, some had gargoyles,

146

some had cherubic children in scant robes.   They were three or four stories high, had windows in the front and back, and usually had skylights on top. Some had shop fronts with pastries, cigarettes, magazines, groceries, etc. The narrow, winding cobble -stone streets begged you to go around the corner to see what came next. I felt like the Parisians were more sophisticated than our New Yorkers, and on this walk it dawned on me that it was due to their being surrounded by such a grand environment.

When I arrived at the cafè, I had to wait for half an hour for Josephine. Patience was not my virtue. So, I bided my time by drinking a cup of espresso. As in every other Parisian cafè, the man behind the bar served the espresso in a small white china cup along with a matching saucer. Lifting the cup to my mouth, I took a moment to savor its pungent smell. Silently, I sighed to myself, "Aah." With the first sip, I experienced an immediate jolt. My taste buds screamed. Only cigarettes (which I didn't smoke anymore) and chocolate (which I could rarely afford) had such a jarring effect on my senses.

Sipping my coffee, I observed the Parisians as they came in and out, quickly drinking down their espresso while standing at the bar. Clad in a white tee-shirt and white pants, the man behind the bar shared a word with each person. He seemed to know them all. I felt like the customers were coming in for more than a cup of coffee.

I still couldn't get over the fact that I could sit here with everyone else who happened to be White, and no one cared.

Just as I was thinking about purchasing one of the croissants in a glass case, Josephine swooped in with apologies and kisses on both cheeks. What else could I expect from a star?

Josephine didn't have on the heavy makeup she wore on stage. I thought she looked even prettier without it. After we made small talk for a while, she asked, "Why don't you stay in Paris? You'll be appreciated more here. The women in Paris admire me so much they're using a hair-smoothing cream I invented. It's called Baker Fix. And I've heard some ladies lie outside in the sun to brown their skin like mine."

I laughed, "You got to be kidding. Browning their skin and Baker Fix?" After we both chuckled, I said, "People seem to respect me more as an artist here, but I have a daughter and sick parents back home."

"I understand. Sorry to hear about your parents." Josephine threw her boa over her shoulder. "Tell me about yourself, Gussie…how you came up."

Feeling like she really cared, I poured out the story of my humble beginnings in Florida, the marriages, the lost loved ones, the poverty, the difficulty with being recognized as an accomplished artist. Then I asked, "How about you?"

"I came up hard too, Gussie. I was born in St. Louis. My mama did laundry like yours, but she really wanted to make it big in Vaudeville. She did a song-and-dance act with a guy named Eddie Carson. She said he was my father, but I'm not sure. He left when I was so young I hardly remember him. Once my mama showed me his picture. He was very dark-skinned. You see how light I am. I'm sure my real daddy was White."

I thought about my daddy. He was overly strict, but he was always there for us. He even protected me from James Savage

Josephine continued. "We was so poor we hardly had enough to eat, and I only had a couple of changes of clothes, not very clean ones. My mama could do the laundry for everyone else, but not for me. She got a new man after my "father," and she had a daughter by him when I was nine. I had to help make money to feed my baby sister and me and my mama. I cleaned houses. One lady on purpose burnt my hands for puttin' too much soap in the basin. I babysat for rich Whites. They had the nerve to tell me not to kiss their babies. It's amazin' that I still liked myself."

"My mama had me dancin' in the background in some of her vaudeville shows. I knew dancin' was my gift. The gift God gave me. But audiences didn't pay much attention to me. Probably because I was dirty, and my clothes were raggedy.

I dropped out of school in fifth grade. That's why my grammar ain't too good. You just heard me say 'ain't,' even though I try not to. I notice you speak in a high-toned way..."

I explained, "I did make it through Cooper Union College, but most of the courses only dealt with sculpture. I credit my elementary school teacher, Mr. Johnson, for my English."

Josephine said, "Even though I made it to fifth grade, I wasn't there most of the time. I'm surprised I can read and write at all."

She crossed her legs, took a dainty drink of her espresso, and said, "At one point, I left my house. I couldn't stand my mama no more. I was homeless. I danced on the streets to make money."

Tears welled up in my eyes. "Josephine, you had it so rough."

She took out a cigarette, put it into a fancy holder, and said, "People who've had it the toughest become the strongest."

Shaking my head in disagreement, I said, "That's not true of everyone. You are special."

Josephine smiled at my compliment. She took a drag of her cigarette and said, "As strong as I tried to be, I wanted a roof over my head, nice clothes, and regular food. When an older man came along and promised me the world, I married him. I was only fourteen. In no time, I didn't like the guy. He was missin' some teeth and drank too much. I didn't want him to touch me, and you know that doesn't go over

149

well with men. In a year, we split up. Then I had another quick marriage that didn't work out. Eventually I made just enough money to get to New York like all us Negroes lookin' for a better life."

"Like me."

"Like you."

"I was a backup dancer for someone in that show 'Shuffle Along.'"

"That musical everyone's seen but me," I said in a self-pitying way.

"Hey, don't feel sorry for yourself. You're an up and comin' artist in Paris now."

I laughed. With all the troubles Josephine faced, she didn't waste much time feeling sorry for herself.

"One night I had my chance to go on. I replaced a dancer who was sick. I hammed it up like you saw me with all my funny faces and wild dancin'. The audience loved me, and the manager wanted me to dance every night."

"What brought you to Paris?"

"I don't know if you realize it, but I danced first in Germany."

"But I thought the Germans were prudish," I said.

"They needed a way to unwind. They were as depressed as we were with all their boys dyin' in the war. I got into a Follies group and was a big hit. When I did the Charleston, the crowds loved me. When I danced with only a halter- top and a banana skirt, they went wild. Ever since then, everyone wants me to dance in a banana skirt."

I smiled but thought that was a little below Josephine's level. "So, what made you leave and come to Paris?"

"That wicked Hitler got popular and forbade people from seein' my shows…along with other things."

"Hitler? I never heard of Hitler."

150

"Adolph Hitler. I hope someone stops him. He's full of evil and hatred—especially against the Jews. I'd heard Paris was very open-minded. So, I came here. As you can see, they've welcomed me with open arms."

With a face that probably exuded idol worship, I said, "I admired you so much when I saw you dance. You're so confident and comfortable with your body."

"That just comes naturally to me. I don't know why."

I hardly told anyone of my fantasy, but I felt so comfortable with Josephine. "I hope you don't mind me sharing this with you, but maybe you would understand, since you're a very successful person. Sometimes I dream I'm climbing stairs to some kind of success. I've always wanted…needed… to sculpt things out of clay. I just have to do it, like eating or sleeping. I think my sculpting will bring me success, but sometimes I'm not so sure."

Josephine looked very serious. "The desire for success is a strange thing. It can bring us high…or low. Success ain't always what it's cracked up to be."

A man interrupted us by coming up to Josephine and asking her for her autograph. She wrote her name on a paper napkin and handed it to him quickly.

Then Josephine continued, "If you ask me, you're probably a really talented sculptor if you're gettin' these scholarships. As for me, I'm doin' great now as a dancer, but I'm only 23. I just started my life. Eventually, I won't be such a cute dancer. Then I'll do other things."

I pondered this for a while. "After the Fontainebleau injustice, I thought I was called to speak out for our people to be treated as equals to Whites."

"How did you like that?"

"I didn't really. I'm not a Garvey or DuBois. But if an injustice happens that involves me, I'll speak the truth." I sipped the last of my coffee. "I 'm 38 now. Older than you. I have to make things happen **now**."

Choking on her coffee, Josephine said, "You're still young! Mark my words, Gussie Savage, you will go on to accomplish even more, in your forties, if not sooner."

Two women walked eagerly towards our table with paper and pens in hand. She motioned to them to wait for her by the door. Then she stood up, adjusted the boa around her neck and lamented. "Before more people bother me, let me say this has been an enjoyable mornin' talkin' with you. I'll watch your career from across the ocean, and you watch mine. I'm sure we'll be readin' about each other. And hopefully we'll see each other again someday."

I stood up as Josephine readied herself to go. I hoped maybe we could do something together again. Josephine was a lot more fun than Elizabeth Prophet. However, on our parting, Josephine just gave me a quick hug and a double kiss like the French did. "Don't forget. Let's keep our eyes out for each other across the miles."

"*Adieu*," I said, as I used one of my French words. Although I said goodbye, I had a strong feeling I would see Josephine again. My mama called it a premonition. She said that whenever you got a premonition you should listen to it.

I hoped I would see Josephine again. It was great talking with her. However, I didn't understand why she questioned the value of success.

TWENTY-TWO

Since I didn't hear back from Irene about The Depression, I thought all was well back home. I was proud of what I'd accomplished—creating about eighteen sculptures in twenty-four months. In Paris, I had the opportunity and money to try new things. This was a wonderful opportunity because in New York, I only received commissions to do busts. I was confident that my new whimsical sculptures and Dahomean pieces would be well received.

Two months after meeting with Josephine, it was time for me to leave. I began packing and figuring out how to ship my works. Then I received a telegram from Irene. It simply said, "Granddaddy is dead."

It was hard to take in. Even though my father had been sick, weak and helpless for some time, I remembered him as Mr. Strong Man. I sent a telegram with money to Irene. "Will be home as soon as I can book a ship. Use this money to bury your beloved grandfather."

Guilt enveloped me. I had left behind Irene and my parents to seek my own happiness in Paris. Now it seemed wrong that I had agreed to let Irene shoulder the burden. And I wasn't there for Daddy in his last hours.

The ocean voyage gave me a couple of weeks to reminisce about my father—how he'd filled my child's heart with fear when he hated my animal sculptures, how he he'd softened when he saw my Mary statue, how he'd inspired our church people in Green Cove Springs and West Palm Beach, and how he'd worked so hard to feed our family. More than anything, I remembered him as a man with firm convictions who would lash out in anger if he thought people were doing wrong. For the first time, I realized how much I was like my daddy. This was a good thing when it came to speaking up for my race, but it could be a bad thing, too.

Part Four

TWENTY-THREE

After our ship docked In New York City, I took a cab home. It was 1931. In the cab ride through the wealthy part of Manhattan, I noticed that some men stood on corners with rumpled business suits and tin cups, and children sold apples. Not everyone looked forlorn, but something bad had happened.

Harlem wasn't what it used to be either. People dragged their feet and wore disappointed scowls. Just two years ago my neighbors walked with a swagger like they expected better things.

While I was gone, some of my family had come to our apartment, brought Daddy to an undertaker, and used our money to bury him at a cemetery. Now Irene and my mother were alone.

As I entered the foyer of our building, I noticed changes. Over the last two years, the mailboxes had tarnished, the floors had hardly been mopped, the overhead fixture missed one of its two light bulbs, and the stairway contained bits of rubbish.

I knocked on our door, but it took a while for someone to answer. Finally, my mother opened it and, after a big hug and shared tears about Daddy, she hobbled back to her usual position on the couch. Irene sat listening to the radio and gave me a quick hello. I expected the deep freeze.

I commented, "Things have changed in New York. What's going on?"

"Didn't you hear about the Stock Market Crash last year?" my daughter asked sarcastically as if I was the dumbest person on earth.

"I read a little about it in the Parisian papers, but people I knew didn't talk about it much. Of course, I was traveling a lot."

"If you would of written more, I would of told you." Irene's tone was full of venom.

Like a child apologizing to her mother, I said, "I was waiting for you to write more. Anyhow, I asked about that thing called The Depression, and you never mentioned it."

Irene let out a disgusted sigh.

"Ladies, ladies," my mother said with firmness, but sadness. "You be mother and daughter. Don't fight. Love on each other."

Irene's shoulders relaxed, and mine did, too. I guessed we still needed my mother.

Mama continued, "About that Stock Market thing, we Coloreds been livin' in poverty so long, we can deal with it. But now that the Whites have to do without, they can't take it."

Thawing out a little but not looking at me, Irene commented, "They say the rich people who lost everything jumped from their tall buildings or shot themselves. Can you imagine?"

It took Irene a few days to warm up more. I wasn't surprised. Even though I would always feel guilty about her, I remembered my vow after Robert and Roberta died. I would take care of myself and do what I wanted inasmuch as possible. Otherwise, I would wither away and die. I had to go to Paris and take advantage of that scholarship.

TWENTY-FOUR

The rest of the U.S. might feel down on their luck, but not me. I was full of hope. *I'll get us out of this dingy tenement in no time,* I thought. The Argent Gallery in Manhattan was delighted when I asked them to display my work. "You're one of our most famous artists in New York City," they told me. "We'll send a delivery truck to pick up your sculptures."

Even if others in Harlem lost theirs, I got a swagger in my step. I found myself humming the latest tunes. I was sure my works from France would sell.

A week without sales was disappointing, a month distressing, six months humiliating. My swagger turned into a shuffle. When the gallery manager called me ever so nicely and wanted me to come in, I knew the little hitch in his voice meant my show was over. He tried to explain. "I'm so sorry, Miss Savage. Your work is magnificent, but people who could afford good art are broke now or overly cautious."

He didn't say the other thing that might be a factor. Possibly, the few who were buying only wanted depictions of White people.

As I walked out of the Argent Gallery on that miserable December morning. I lamented, *There is no way I can win now, even if I create the best art in the world.* A fury stronger than the freezing winter wind took hold of me. I felt my heart turn savage again, bursting with rage. I didn't want to bring it home to my poor mother and daughter. Instead, I went to nearby Central Park and found a secluded area. On one side was a retaining wall and on another was a small hill. I sat down on a bench behind a bushy pine tree in this little alcove. No one could see me.

I yelled, "Why, God? This is so unfair. I do the best work of my life, and it's really good. Then the stock market crashes and I can't sell it." I stood up, grabbed a branch from a tree, and snapped it over my knee. "Why? Why, Lord, have you sentenced me and the rest of us Negroes to a life of poverty? If my people had money, they would buy my art. If I had money, my life wouldn't be so hard." I took a rock and threw it against the wall. I screamed, "Take me, God, take me right now to my heavenly home! Just take me! Take me!"

A man's voice called sheepishly from the other side of the wall, "Are you all right, Miss?"

I answered in a shaky voice, "I... I'm okay."

"Are you sure, Ma'am?" The guy's words were laced with compassion.

"I'm sure," I sobbed.

I scurried away in a direction where the concerned man couldn't see me. This was so embarrassing, but at least I had vented part of my rage. I hurried towards the stop for the Harlem bus. I bent over double to fight the wind's violent assault. The effort helped calm my savage heart, but not completely. On the crowded ride home, I grabbed an overhead strap tightly. With the state I was in, I hated being jammed in so close to others. I felt like jabbing them and yelling, *Get away from me*!

When I arrived home, Irene was out. My mama sat on our sofa, listening to her favorite radio show. Shivering, I took off my coat and boots and tried to go to my room as quickly as possible.

"Hello, Gussie. Why you in such a hurry? Look at me, Baby."

I turned to Mama, and she could see my face was stained with tears. "Come here, Gussie, and sit by your mama."

I hardly ever shared a moment of closeness with Mama. When I was a kid, she was always busy with the little ones. When she moved in with us, I felt I should take care of her. The truth was, though, that when I was blue I longed to get lost in her loving arms.

She had me sit right next to her and put her right arm around my shoulders. "What's wrong, Baby?" That's all it took for me to unleash my tears. Mama kept her arm around me as I told her the story about my sculptures not selling and my theory that it was partly because of the Depression but mainly because the sculptures depicted our people. Mama kept saying, "It'll be all right, Baby."

Between sobs, I cried, "It's so unfair! I go all the way to Paris, study under France's greatest artists, make the best work of my life, and it still does no good!"

Mama said, "There be nothing I can do to relieve your suffering. We don't get to pick the color of our skin. But look at all you 'complished and how the world done took notice of you just like the omens said. Don't give up, Baby. It won't be long til you have more success."

Finally, I stopped crying.

Mama took my chin in her hand. She looked at me and said, "No matter what happens to any of us, we have to wipe our eyes and keep goin.' Look for what's beautiful in life, help each other out, and love the Lord. That's all we can do."

Mama's words and her arm around my shoulders comforted me. "Thank you, Mama. I love you." Then I went to my room.

TWENTY-FIVE

Countee Cullen stayed in Paris a few months after I came back. When he returned, he called me. "I'm in New York for a while. I heard about your father. I'm so sorry." He sounded like he truly was feeling my pain. "How about if I round up our crowd and we come to your place again? Maybe it will get your mind off your loss for a while."

I knew my voice was less than enthusiastic, but I said, "Come. It will be nice to see everyone." And they came.

Countee arrived first. He was still so dapper and positive. However, this time he had some bad news for me. In the kitchen, he said Joe Gould had contacted him.

"Oh, no!" I shrieked so loudly that my mother called from the bedroom, "What's the matter, Gussie?"

"Everything's okay, Mama. Don't worry."

I said to Countee, "Just whisper."

"Joe says that he was in a mental asylum while you were gone and that you had told everyone about it, thereby ruining his reputation."

"Huh? I can't believe it. I thought I'd gotten away from that lout. I didn't know he was in an asylum, but that's where he belongs."

Countee smiled and put his hand on my shoulder. "Okay, let's forget about it tonight, and you just have a nice time."

It took me a minute, but I settled myself down. When the others came, they offered their condolences about my father and then asked me about my studies in Paris.

160

Within no time, though, the conversation turned to a group called the Harmon Foundation. I knew about the foundation before I went to Paris. Its goal was to encourage Negro artists by exhibiting their work. In fact, they once exhibited one of my works, partly because the very first Harmon shows were at my beloved 135th St. Library. A woman named Mary Beattie Brady organized many of the exhibits, but while Mr. Harmon was alive, there were checks and balances on her. When Mr. Harmon died, Mary Beattie Brady took over all the foundation's activities.

Langston said, "The problem is that Brady decides whose art the foundation exhibits, even though she has no artistic background.

Gwendolyn Bennett said, "That wouldn't be so bad if she had Negro and even White art authorities to assist her. She just consults with Whites who have no training in the arts."

"That doesn't sound fair," I scowled.

Anne Bennis, a new librarian at our library, had been quiet all evening, but this subject made her pipe up. "I don't understand either what gives Brady the right to say whose work is good and whose isn't."

I filed this in the back of my mind. What Brady was doing seemed wrong. However, out of self-interest, I thought someday I would contact her. Perhaps she would like and exhibit my newer work—even if she was unfair. If she gave me guff, I would stand up to her.

Soon, though, I got too busy to think about Brady and the Harmon Foundation. Dr. Walter Crump wanted me to do his bust. He heard about me from James Weldon Johnson. James told me that Dr. Crump was a White physician who would do anything to give our people a hand up. He sponsored scholarships for Negroes to the university where he taught.

James arranged for Dr. Crump to come to my apartment. I was ashamed of the miserable shape of our building, but the good doctor didn't seem to mind. He loved my mother (who wouldn't?), and he made friendly conversation with Irene. He sat for me a number of times and was a pleasant, intelligent gentleman. When I completed his bust, he said he loved it. I think I captured the twinkle of kindness in his eyes along with a quiet expression of wisdom in the set of his mouth. Dr. Crump had the bust cast in bronze to be displayed at his university. Oh, how I wished that all my clay sculptures would be cast in bronze. Then they wouldn't turn to dust!

The amount Dr. Crump paid me kept me from returning to laundry work, at least for a while. Then I got a call from a man named Millen Brand. I don't know how he got my phone number, but he sounded like a nice enough person. He said he'd like to meet me and perhaps have me do a bust of him. So, I arranged to meet him at the library.

A slender, young White man with a full smile, Brand told me he was writing a book about the experiences of people in mental hospitals. He said his wife who was a poet had associated with a man for a while who had been in a mental hospital—none other that Joe Gould. She introduced Joe to her husband.

My body stiffened.

That's how Brand heard about me. I guess Gould displayed his initially charming manner and drew in Brand. He gave him a sob story about how I had rebuffed him after returning from Paris. Of course, I had rejected him long before then, but Brand didn't know it. Gould begged Brand to arrange a meeting between him and me.

I probably disturbed the people studying nearby as I ranted, "Joe Gould has come close to ruining my life. Everywhere I go, everything I do he

162

tries to insert himself into it! If my doing your bust was nothing but a ploy to satisfy Joe Gould, I don't want the job."

I stood up. Brand stood up too.

"I'm sorry to upset you, Miss Savage. I didn't know he creates so much misery for you. Please, sit down. I really do want you to make a bust of me, and I'll tell Joe Gould to leave you alone."

When Brand contacted Gould and told him not to bother me, the evil man started sending Brand letters with horrible comments about me as well as Brand's wife. He called Brand at 4:30 one morning, yelling all kinds of obscenities.

Brand went to the police and looked into pressing charges against him. Gould begged him not to. Brand met Gould under an arch in Washington Square. He agreed to drop charges if Gould promised to never talk to him or his wife again and to stop pursuing me. Gould agreed. That was the last Millen Brand and his wife heard from Joe. I doubted that I would be so lucky. I would have gone to the police, but I didn't think the police would put themselves out to protect a poor, Negro woman living in Harlem.

By this time Millen and I were on a first name basis. As he had requested initially, Millen had me do his bust. It took eight sittings. Towards the end, an ear fell off. I joked, "Now we'll have to start over." Millen looked concerned, then laughed, knowing by then I cold be a teaser.

So, Millen came in for an extra evening of posing to build up his ear. From my studio, we heard my mother listening to a scary radio show. The drama was heightened, because with radio you could only hear the sounds, of course, and not see what was happening. When I completed his ear, Millen wanted to stay longer and sit in the living room with my mother and me to hear the end of the show. After it was over, he jotted down the story so his wife—who was deaf—could read it. Millen was such a sweet man.

"You have a lovely little family here," Millen said as he left.

TWENTY-SIX

Since I had Brand's payment for his bust, I still didn't have to go back to laundry work. I had some rare free time. So, I decided to take on Mary Brady. I would see if she would exhibit at least one of my newer works.

I sent a letter asking for the privilege of displaying my work in one of the Harmon exhibits. She replied that the foundation only accepted work that had been completed within the last year and asked if my pieces had been done less than a year ago. That seemed like a ridiculous rule, but I remained polite and sent a new letter requesting that my Parisian creations be accepted. I said I had completed them about a year ago. Brady replied with a question, "Do you have them dated? Send me a letter with the exact dates of when you created them."

Unfortunately, I had put the exact dates on the back of the works, and I sculpted them a year and a half or two years earlier. When I opened Brady's return letter, I shouted, "What?"

I called her. "Miss Brady, I received your letter that my almost new Parisian works were rejected. Why is there such a strict one-year rule?"

With a voice as cold as ice, she said, "We must have such rules or else we would have too many pieces to consider."

"Ooookay," I drew out the word with full sarcasm. Then I couldn't restrain myself. "One more thing. Some of my peers and I are not happy that you have no Negro judges—either formally educated or experienced with the arts."

That was the death knell for me.

"You are a troublemaker, Miss Savage. Years ago you could have handled that whole Fontainebleau thing better. You embarrassed the decision-making committee, and now you are meeting with artists who call into question the rules of the Harmon Foundation. I want nothing to do with the likes of you. This phone call is over."

I was thunderstruck. This was the fulfillment of my worst fears. Did my railing against the art establishment ten years ago lead to my being ostracized? Had influential people been talking behind my back, labeling me as a "troublemaker?" Was my past the ruin of my career in the present?

This time my heart didn't lash out in rage. I didn't throw anything or break anything. I didn't scream, "Why me, God?" I was simply in a state of shock.

As always, my mother was home. She had heard me talking on the phone. "What is it, Gussie? What were you sayin' about a one-year rule? You look like you done seen a ghost."

"It's nothing, Mama. I'm just sad that one of my works isn't getting into a show."

I smiled wanly and went to my room.

"I'll be right here on this couch if you need me, Baby."

"I know," I said through my closed door.

This blow left me feeling more helpless than agitated. Now those steps up the staircase sure didn't look like they were leading to artistic success.

For two weeks, I pretty much stayed in my room lying on my bed letting my mind go wherever it wanted and not thinking much—like when John and Robert died. Then one day Irene got mad and barked, "Why are you laying around? Am I the only one who has to work?"

It was a hot summer day. In fact, I had been sweating in bed. Irene's complaint snapped me out of my lethargy. I went outside and sat on the steps.

I'd quit smoking when I went to Paris, but thought I might as well take it up again as soon as I could get a pack. I watched the people go by. Many said "hi" as they passed. Some asked me where I'd been. I realized people in the neighborhood knew me and liked me. After all, I'd lived in Harlem for around ten years. Then it dawned on me. I am an artist of the people—people like me who are poor and came up the hard way. That's my strength. *How can I share my talent with them*? Forget the Big Shots.

I went back into our apartment, washed up, and put on a clean dress. When night fell, I listened with my mother to one of her mysteries. She said, "You look better, Gussie."

The morning after my revelation about being an artist of my people—specifically my people in Harlem—I got up in a good mood, ate a decent breakfast and sat on the steps again. The weather on this bright August morning was perfect. The way the sun hit the brick of the buildings gave them an orange glow. The knife sharpeners with their pushcarts, the sweet potato man, and the peanut vendor all had the dignity of The Water Seller of Seville in Velazquez' painting. I imagined that I really was in Seville or some other picturesque European city.

As I sat on the step mulling over what I could do to share my artistic talent, I was shocked to see a boy swaggering down the street like the boy I had once sculpted—David. As he got closer, I stood up. I just about screamed. "It's you! About a foot taller!"

In what was probably a demanding tone, I asked, "What happened to you?"

David opened his mouth in surprise and then smiled. He gave me a rare hug. "I hated to just leave without saying goodbye, but the police stopped by where me and the guys hung out, and they wanted to bust me. They said I stole a loaf of bread from a store."

"'What?'" I asked like I couldn't believe it, but I knew David could be desperate enough.

"Sometimes when the hunger was too strong, I had to steal food. I just had to."

I nodded in sympathy.

"You know, Miss Savage, it seems mean that most people can have food, and the rest of us can't."

"I understand, David. It does seem unfair," I said with the experience of one who had suffered her share of hunger pangs. "So, what happened next?"

"They told me they'd have to book me at the police station. I been in jail before, and I couldn't stand being cooped up. While they took out the handcuffs, we heard two cars bang into each other at the corner. The cops looked the way of the crash, and I took off runnin.' One of 'em tried to catch me, but he tripped, and I ran round a building and got away. As fast as I could, I ran and walked all the way to Central Park so they wouldn't find me."

"That's a long, long way from Harlem. What did you do in Central Park?"

"I found a little spot where some homeless folk hid. Stayed with them for a year or so. Came to look for you, but you been gone, I guess."

"I studied in Paris for two years."

"Aren't you the lucky one?" David smiled. He could have been jealous, but he looked sincerely happy for me. He knew I had struggled, too.

I told him how nice it was to see him again and to keep in touch.

David kept coming by after this, and we'd talk about whatever was new. Thinking about him and the good people of Harlem, I said to him one day, "I've been trying to figure out how I can bring art to our people."

"You mean like start an art school or something?"

I must have looked at David like he told me I won the lottery, because he asked, "What? What you so excited about?"

"You gave me a great idea. I will start an art studio in our neighborhood. I'll start it right here, in my apartment upstairs, and then maybe I'll get a storefront or something."

David said, "That sounds fine, Miss Savage," but his heart wasn't in it. "Well, I better be goin'."

"Not so fast, David. Would you like to be my first student?"

"I like you, Miss Savage, but I'm no good at art, and I ain't really interested in it. You give me a broke radio or vacuum, and I'd love fixin' it. But art, no. There's some kids on the streets, though, who like to paint things on walls."

"Ah, those are the kinds of kids I'm interested in."

"Great, Miss Savage, I'll bring a couple 'round tomorrow. But I got to warn you—they smell. Like me."

I laughed. "That's fine, but you and them bring an appetite. I'll make peach cobbler."

The next day I waited on the front steps. By now, I'd bought cigarettes and was smoking again. Although my talk with David gave me hope, my stomach still churned from feeling rejected by the art establishment. I thought maybe smoking could settle it down. I clung to any kind of lifeline to keep me afloat.

At around 11am, David showed up with two boys. They looked about his age. One was maybe 5 foot 6, but still looked very young. The other was probably under 5 foot . Their clothes were tattered, and their faces were dirty, but when David introduced us, they both said they liked art.

I brought the boys upstairs. My mother was lying on the couch, but sat up when we entered. "Oh, hello," she said. As I led them into the kitchen for their peach cobbler, I turned towards her and said, "Remember I mentioned that some boys might come over for art lessons?"

"Oh, yes," she said in the brightest of tones, "Glad to have the boys."

The pan of peach cobbler disappeared in no time. "Very good," one said. "Thank you," said the other. "I told you Miss Savage is special," David added.

I smiled at David. "Thanks for the compliment, but since you're not interested in art, I'll let you go. Come back and visit again soon, though."

"Catch ya later," David's voice was strong, like he was proud of making all this happen.

After I put away the dishes, I transformed my kitchen into a studio. I laid out large pieces of paper with pencils. I taught the two boys about shading and perspective. Then I said, "Draw whatever you like."

They drew like they were in a frenzy— they loved this as much as gobbling down the peach cobbler. One boy drew the skyscrapers in Manhattan in an interesting, abstract way. The other sketched a realistic, well-proportioned face of a dog with his tongue hanging out. It was apparent the boys had talent and desire.

The next day they brought two more of their friends. My daughter was off from work, and when they weren't looking, she held her nose. Poor Irene. The fellas looked and smelled like the street kids they were, but they were polite and respectful.

My apartment was full of sculptures I made, but couldn't sell. The boys were spellbound by them. At least, they appreciated my artistry.

But I was asking too much of my mother and daughter to put up with a constant parade of strangers. I went to see my new friend, the librarian Anne Bennis. After I told her what I was doing, she advised me, "Why don't you write a grant for money from The Carnegie Foundation? They fund worthwhile community projects with positive goals."

That was the same group that gave me a grant to do my three-week study of art in several European countries. I filled out the application, and in it I asked for funds to start a storefront school to teach art to

170

poor children. Much to my delight, they gave me the money. It was a whole $1,500! The Carnegie Corporation came through again.

I got a basement apartment on 143rd St. and put out a sign, "The Savage Studio of Arts and Crafts."

While mostly teenage girls and boys came to my studio, I sometimes had older students. Once I worked with a 21-year-old, young man named Norman Lewis. Slender and serious, Norman was a presser at a nearby tailor and dry cleaning store. He told me he observed that I left dusty footprints coming in and out. Somehow he got the idea I was a sculptor. He wanted to see where my footprints led, and he followed them to my basement studio. When he looked into the window, he could see people drawing and sculpting. He knocked on the door and asked if he could paint at my studio. Of course, I welcomed him in.

Norman talked about how his parents gave all their attention to his older brother who was an accomplished musician. His father told him art is "a White man's profession and hence you're wasting your time." Because of my history with the art establishment, I wanted to tell Norman his father was right. Nevertheless, I knew Norman was driven to paint, and I could not discourage him.

After the younger students left for the day, Norman would stay until his hand got too tired to hold a brush. We often got into boisterous arguments. I found myself becoming more outspoken, and Norman was the same way. He was impressed with famous artists from the past and, before meeting me, he had somehow earned money to buy a variety of books about artists such as El Greco, Michelangelo and Monet. He felt he could learn to paint by copying their work or their style. I told him it would be best to first learn the basics of art, the formal elements, like I did at Cooper Union. Norman didn't agree. A real know-it-all, he always thought he was smarter than me. I handled his challenges like I did Irene's. I tried to intimidate him with quick, loud retorts. I would never back down on an argument with Norman.

Once Norman challenged me, "What makes you think you know so much? You aren't a real sculptor. Your sculptures are all in clay. A real sculptor would have her work bronzed or would sculpt with marble."

This comment pierced my heart. It got to my big problem: Poverty. A problem I didn't want to admit. I felt a tear roll down my cheek and quickly wiped it away.

Norman must have noticed. In an unusually soft tone, he asked, "What's wrong, Miss Savage? You're usually so quick with a comeback."

As hard as it was for me, I admitted, "I've never had the money to buy marble, and I can't afford to have my sculptures cast in bronze. My works will crumble with time."

"I'm so sorry," Norman stuttered, "I...I... thought you had money, since you're a famous artist."

I turned my back to him, went to the sink, and washed my hands. I spoke coldly, not wanting to admit my disappointment with life. "Keep on painting, Norman. Your luck might be better than mine." I added under my breath, "Just don't cross the art establishment."

Puzzled, Norman looked back at his latest work and never criticized me again.

Sometimes Norman got so involved with painting that he would stay until two or three in the morning. I never locked up until the last student left. So, I would stay with him. He did a painting of a man brought low by the Depression bending over a container of hot coals. I loved that painting.

A couple years after he left the studio, he came back to tell me, "You know, Miss Savage, my rejection of formal study by you may have slowed my development as an artist."

My mind went back to another one of my older students—Kenneth Clark. He came to me at the age of seventeen. Fresh out of high school, he had a variety of aspirations, and one was to become an artist. His single mother was a seamstress at a nearby laundry and had organized a union for seamstresses. She was a go-getter, that's for sure. She wanted Kenneth to get a good education and not be stuck doing menial work. Kenneth thought he would like sculpting. So, his mother encouraged him to come to my school. One day he was trying to do a nude sculpture of a woman from the waist up. I didn't use unclothed models. Some of the boys were so young that they wouldn't keep a straight face.

Kenneth was looking at a picture of a dressed woman in a book. Then he started looking at Gwendolyn Knight, the girl sitting next to him. Gwendolyn said, "Quit looking at me."

I came over to Kenneth and said, "You're having trouble with the breast, aren't you?"

Sheepishly, he said, "Yes."

In the name of art, I opened my blouse and showed him my breast. Gwendolyn opened her eyes in shock, then laughed. Kenneth took it all in and sculpted away.

Eight years later when Kenneth came to visit me, he was an up-and-coming social psychologist who, along with his wife, studied how children reacted to each another on the basis of race. We had quite a laugh recounting my...shall we say?... openness.

Speaking of Gwendolyn Knight, this lovely girl with a beautiful accent came to me when she graduated from high school. Slowly but surely, she told me of how she was born in Barbados and how her mother allowed a friend of hers to take her to the United States for a better life. Gwendolyn was only seven at the time and had not seen her mother since. She found out about my studio when, on her way to her waitress job, she looked inside the basement windows and saw what we were doing. Like most of us, she had the hunger to create art. She liked to do large- scale line drawings on paper. Gwendolyn always listened with respect to me, and she seemed to see me as the mother she didn't have.

TWENTY-SEVEN

My own mother's health started deteriorating. She had difficulty breathing, her legs swelled up, and she was always tired. When I took her to the nearby Harlem Hospital, the doctor told us she had Congestive Heart Failure; her heart was tired and wasn't beating hard enough to bring sufficient blood to her body. She would not die right away, but we could anticipate a rapid decline in her breathing and overall health.

Irene took it as hard as I did. Her grandma was the mother I wasn't. We fawned over Mama as much as we could with our busy lives, but my mother didn't want a lot of attention. She slowly left the world with the attitude she had all her life—not expecting too much, looking for the least bit of beauty, and trusting the Good Lord. When she passed, we buried her next to Daddy. Although we had time to prepare ourselves for Mama's departure, I missed her every day after she left this earth. Mama was the one who believed in me as a child, and she was the one who recently let this big baby rest my head on her shoulder.

At night as I lay in bed trying to fall asleep, I felt my mother's presence. I went to her with my everyday problems. As always, she listened well and, at times, gave me advice...although silently now.

Shortly after Mama's passing, Irene talked about a young man she met at the laundry. Irene was grown by now and came and went as she pleased. She said she'd been seeing this guy for some time but hadn't mentioned it. Like when she was little, she didn't share much with me.

The man's name was Julius, and she suspected he'd be proposing any day. As a result, she'd be moving out. Usually she and I only spoke about practical things. So, I'm sure it must have been hard for her to ask in a most gentle way, "You'll be all right on your own, won't you? I know we both miss Grandma." For a change, my daughter shared how she felt, "I miss Grandma so much that I cry every night."

"I know. I hear you, and I feel sad for you," I interjected. While I was having silent conversations with Mama, Irene was crying in the next bedroom. Again, maybe I was a bad mother. I heard Irene cry, but I was so lost in my own grief that I didn't go to comfort her.

Irene continued, "Maybe getting married will help me feel better, but I don't feel right about leaving you…at least not now."

I didn't want to show weakness, and I didn't want to hold Irene back from happiness. So, I looked away from her and out the window. "Miss you? I have so much work. I'm very busy. Don't think twice about it."

It didn't seem like I fooled Irene, though. She walked over to me and put her hand on my shoulder—the closest thing to a hug that I'd had from her for a long time. When I turned towards her, she gave me a worried smile and walked slowly towards the door to go see Julius.

That night I felt like Mama sent me a message: Sometimes you're too hard on yourself when it comes to Irene. Look at how you were willing to let her go, even if you'd rather have her company.

However, luck didn't go Irene's way. Two weeks later she came home from her laundry shift at 10PM. I was sitting in the living room listening to the radio. Irene announced she found out Julius was cheating.

'Ugh!" she groaned loudly. "My best friend at work said she saw him twice at a bar getting all lovey with another woman. I guess I won't be leaving."

With that Irene asked, "Would you mind if I took this?" She unplugged the radio and brought it to her room, closing the door behind her.

I stood by the door and said, "I feel bad for you, Irene. Is there anything I can do?"

"No, I'll be okay," she said in a mournful voice.

I talked with Mama about it that night, and I felt she told me to give Irene special care during this rough time and not to worry about her, because she was doing just fine up in heaven. That was the last specific message I ever got from Mama, but I still talked to her for years. She was always a good listener.

After the breakup, Irene cried twice as hard at night. I'd go to her bedroom door and ask if she'd like me to sit with her by her bed, but she always said, "Thanks anyhow, Mom, but I've got to deal with this myself." Shades of how I talked with my neighbor Cynthia after destroying my sculptures just days ago. Maybe my daughter and I were more alike than I thought.

It seemed, though, that Irene's feelings for this Julius guy didn't run too deep. Within about two months, she said she was over him and she went back to her normal self.

TWENTY- EIGHT

As much as I loved teaching, I found that the grant money for my art school didn't pay my bills. Luckily, I still received commissions for busts. I was always happier having my hands full of clay instead of laundry suds.

A man named Major Edward Bowes had a hit radio show called "The Amateur Hour". His show was the most widely listened to on the radio. He gave opportunities to Negro people to sing, and he started many famous people on the road to success—even a little Italian guy named Frank Sinatra. Somehow Major Bowes heard of my reputation and commissioned me to do his bust. Seeing as how he was very busy, I went to his radio studio to work on it. He had an ordinary, but confident, face and wore his thinning hair like most aging White men of our day— slicked back with something like Brylcreem. I enjoyed his genial personality, and he paid me well.

Then, I was asked by a musician named Ted Upshure to do his bust. I consented at one of his parties. Ted loved to entertain. Like me, he was the child of parents who were slaves as children and, like me, he scratched and clawed to get an education in what he loved best. In his case, it was music. Somehow he made it to Julliard. After a couple of drinks, I said I would do his bust, even though Ted never had enough money for anything, and I knew I wouldn't get paid much. With the knowledge that Ted had to work at menial jobs to survive as a musician, I captured his many wrinkles, but I think I also depicted the playful glint in his eyes that said, "I'm going to enjoy life and do what I love best." When I completed his bust, Ted said he wouldn't have any money to pay me for about six months. So, I had Anne Bennis exhibit it at the library for a while, and then it was in a gallery. This is where Fate came knocking again. Someone important saw the bust, admired it, and brought it to the attention of The National Association of Women Painters and Sculptors. I was elected as the first Negro to be a part of the group. Finally some recognition from the White art establishment!

This honor and my recent commissions got me dreaming again about climbing that staircase to success. I fantasized in great detail about what my room at the top of the stairs would look like. It would be large and ornate. A variety of people would be present. Rich and Poor, White and Colored would mingle as equals. All would admire my *Dahomean Women*, my portrait busts of famous people, and especially my *Gamin* sculpture. They would appreciate the depth and beauty of my Negro subjects, and they would actually purchase my work.

Suddenly, a knock on the door disturbed my bliss. I asked, "Who's there?"

"It's me. Alice Neel."

Alice was a fellow artist, and I'd always liked her. Tall, white, large-boned, and usually wearing her hair in a style like a man's, she was an artist who had strong opinions to match her imposing demeanor. Yet she also had a heart of gold for anyone who suffered. She had suffered terribly herself. Her Cuban husband kidnapped their little daughter, and Alice had a nervous breakdown, ending up in a mental institution. Recently she'd been coming to poetry group gatherings at my place. During our discussions about politics, she espoused the idea that Communism might be the way to solve inequalities in American society.

When I opened the door, I was eager to see Alice, but she had with her the most despicable creature on earth—Joe Gould. I wanted to shut the door on them.

179

Immediately Alice got to the bottom of why she came. "In the process of posing for a portrait he wanted me to do, Joe told me he hoped I could be a mediator between you and him."

While Alice and I remained standing, Joe finagled his way through us and plopped down onto my couch like he owned it. "Yeah, I paid Alice actual money for that portrait. I asked her to make it somewhat abstract and show me with three penises," Joe laughed. "I'm sure you girls are eager to get any commission you can nowadays."

Alice sneered at Joe with a look that could kill. "I only agreed to the three penises, because I thought they were a symbol of your inflated ego."

In a sharp manner unlike any I had ever used with Alice, I asked, "How in the hell do you know that lout?"

Alice answered meekly, "He was in the mental hospital with me."

I felt my face contort with rage. Looking at me, Alice said in a quivering voice, "I think I made a mistake bringing Joe here."

"Oh, no, you didn't," Joe said lightheartedly. "We could be friends if only Augusta could forgive and forget."

With my jaw clenched, I spat out, "Get out of here, right now! Both of you! You mean well, Alice, but Joe Gould has almost ruined my life."

"I got ya, Augusta," said Alice. Pulling Joe up from the couch, she just about dragged him out of my apartment. When they left, I directed my frenzy towards rubbing a cleaning solvent into my couch to get rid of all remnants of that disgusting Joe Gould.

TWENTY-NINE

My greatest source of joy was still my students. In giving them directions and encouragement, I was usually patient and kind. However, if one of them—like Norman Lewis—challenged my authority or my ability, it was a different matter.

A teenage girl almost made me lose my temper. God knows what her situation was at home. She wore the same clothes every day and was quite skinny. She gravitated to the sculpting table. One day when she was sculpting a small horse, I leaned over to show her how she could use a riffler to file the piece's surface. "Oh, okay," she said, like she couldn't be bothered.

I was an expert at returning sarcasm with sarcasm. "And what makes you think you know so much about sculpting?"

"I'm going to be famous someday and rich—not like you."

"Not like me?"

In a snide way, she said, "I know you live right in Harlem with all us poor people. If you're so great, why didn't you get out?"

At first, I was tongue-tied. Not even Norman was that insulting! I was surprised by what finally came out of my mouth. "I want to be in Harlem. Harlem is my home. I will sculpt our people and give them the dignity we deserve."

From then on, that young girl accepted any help I gave her—sometimes even with a smile.

Teaching art to disadvantaged and lost, but talented, young people might be my true calling. Perhaps I was already at the top of the stairs, and the Savage Studio of Arts and Crafts was the room for which I was destined. It wasn't the fancy room I had

181

recently imagined with all the Whites and Negroes, rich and poor mingling as one. Rather it was a room with all the poor young Negroes whom I saved from the streets and who were now creating beautiful art. I was in the background in this fantasy, and I wasn't making much money, but I felt blessed.

One day a reporter came to interview me and to see what my studio looked like. He was quite impressed with all the students and with how they were so serious about their art.

I told him, "If I can inspire one of these youngsters to develop the talent I know they possess, then my monument will be in their work." He put this quote into the newspaper, and people commented to me that they were inspired by my words.

At about this time The Works Progress Association began. Our country was in such deep depression that President Franklin D. Roosevelt believed he had to do something. According to his radio talks, he didn't just want to put people on the dole; he wanted them to sharpen their job skills or learn new ones. So, he started the WPA to give paid jobs and training to unemployed people. An art program was created to extend relief also to artists, actors, writers, and musicians. Although the arts had never been high on FDR's list of priorities, he felt funding them would provide a double benefit. It would put to work legions of unemployed people with artistic talent, and their work could entertain and enrich the larger population.

Word was that his wife Eleanor, a fervent supporter of the arts, nudged Franklin along. I heard that she was behind the $27 million he said he would distribute to different art centers across the U.S.

I was never so thrilled as when I received a phone call asking if I was willing to run the arts program in Harlem.

"What? Really?" I asked so dramatically that Irene turned down the radio and stared at me. When I hung up, I giddily told my daughter about my new position. Aside from the joy the job would bring, I told her I'd get a good, steady paycheck.

Irene was coming out of the kitchen. She smiled widely. "I guess it was worth putting up with those straggly boys you used to bring in."

My studio became the jumping off point for what was titled, "The WPA Harlem Community Art Center." I could tell that the space I had would be nowhere near enough to teach the many young people whom I hoped to recruit. And, so, I arranged for new quarters, hired a couple of assistants, and we put out posters that said, "Free Instruction in Drawing, Sculpting, Printing, Weaving, Lithography Metal Craft, Photography and Costume Illustration."

Interestingly enough, a children's psychiatric ward of a hospital in New York City asked if they could send some of their children to our classes. "Yes, of course," I responded. It was amazing to see how those kids got so absorbed in their artwork that they temporarily found escape from their problems.

Everything was going well. I had never been an administrator, but I was doing lots of planning, bookkeeping and arranging with excellent results. Soon we had a number of storefronts—remodeled, renovated and ready to go. But then a big problem arose. I went back to lamenting, *Why me, Why me, God? Must I always have a problem?*

It had to do with hiring teachers. From teaching and living in Harlem, I knew a number of outstanding Negro artists who would be well qualified to teach our younger generation. However, the government managers turned to Mary Brady and other White people who knew nothing about art to decide who to hire. Why couldn't the WPA respect my judgment? Who had worked harder to educate the talented young adults who could now assume this role? Perhaps most important, why didn't they understand that Negro students would feel more hope for their future if they saw Negroes as their examples for what they could accomplish?

I made my opinions known to the bureaucrats, but it was a fight. I wondered again if my run-ins with the art establishment back in my Fontainebleau days led to this problem. I feared the Big Shots were saying behind my back, "She's nothing but trouble. Don't listen to her."

Still I found great joy in encouraging young talent. One of the most interesting aspects of the Project was the sense of community it built. Creating art could be lonely. By picking up their paychecks every week at the WPA office and working on projects together, the artists felt connected.

One particularly serious boy named Jacob Lawrence really wanted to be part of our Art Center. His parents were divorced, and his mother placed him and two of his siblings in foster homes until she could support them. She moved from Philadelphia to Harlem, got a job as a laundress and then sent for the kids. According to Jacob, she really loved him but worried because he was often depressed. All he wanted to do was draw. He hated school. Jacob eventually dropped out of high school, and so his mother got him into an art program with a famous Negro artist named Charles Alston, who brought Jacob to me.

Alston said, "This kid has a style all his own. No matter how I teach him, he goes back to doing the same kind of art. But I have to admit, Augusta, it is good. He likes to use bold colors and repeat them. He usually does scenes from Harlem and can make the most depressing subject matter enjoyable by using bright, bold colors and abstract designs."

His mother couldn't afford to keep paying Alston for art lessons. The WPA paid our artist-students. If Jacob got into the WPA, he could bring home his much-needed pay to help keep the family afloat.

It turned out that Jacob was only 20, and a student had to be 21 to get into the WPA program. So, Jacob took odd jobs to support himself and his family and forgot about art being a career. On the exact date of his 21st birthday, I sought him out and got him in as a paid student-artist at the WPA. As a result, he had the time, money and materials to devote to his art. Jacob thanked me numerous times saying, "If it wasn't for you, Miss Savage, I'd be washing dishes or working at the docks for the rest of my life."

*****

Life Magazine put my picture on their cover. The accompanying story was titled "Negroes: Their Artists Are Gaining In Skill and Recognition." When my nemesis, Mary Brady, heard that the cover story was in the works, she pleaded with *Life* not to feature me, but they went ahead anyhow. I couldn't have been prouder. I bought every copy of *Life* that I could afford and gave copies to my friends and family. *Perhaps success is now in my hands*, I thought.

For a couple of weeks, I strutted to work like a proud peacock. Gradually, though, my feet dragged.

Anger began welling up in my heart again. Despite my being on the cover of *Life* magazine and my success with administering the art program, the WPA managers still did not hire the people I recommended. Instead, they still listened to Mary Brady.

I wasn't the only artist infuriated with the Harmon foundation and the WPA's reluctance to hire Negro teachers. Elba Lightfoot, an outspoken Negro artist, said to me one day, "We have to do something. The WPA doesn't respect us."

So, she and I and some of our poetry group people met together one night to figure out what we could do. After some discussion, Elba suggested, "Let's form an organization. It can be named whatever we want, and we can write fancy goals, but in reality we can use it to figure out ways to bring respect to our people and get our Negro art exhibited."

We ended up calling it The Harlem Artists Guild, and we met every week to discuss challenges we faced as Negro artists. I was the vice president and eventually the president. Members included Romare Bearden, Gwendolyn Bennett, Aaron Douglas, and Norman Lewis. Of course, writers (who were artists) could also join the guild. By 1937 our membership grew to about 90. We planned our own art exhibitions. Who cared about Brady and her elitist snobs?

One evening, a new person came to our meeting. The newcomer wore a black suit, white shirt, and black bow tie. His skin was a light, golden brown. He had a full mustache, and his hair was thick and wavy.

When we greeted him and asked him to introduce himself, he said, "I am Arturo Alfonso Schomburg. I am a man of Negro but also German descent." He added with a wink and a smile, "I hope you will not let the German part keep me from joining you."

We laughed, and I said, "Certainly not, but what brings you to us tonight?"

He responded, "Let me start with a little story about my background. My mother was a Negro midwife from St. Croix who for better opportunities immigrated to Puerto Rico. My father was a German merchant who often came to Puerto Rico for business. They met somehow and fell in love. My parents were wonderful, and I had a happy childhood, but then I had a terrible experience in grade school. I got a teacher who thought Negroes were of no value. That made me want to learn and tell about the accomplishments of our Negro people."

We were all ears.

He continued, "My teacher said, 'Write a report about someone who did great things and whom you admire. Of course, this will not include Negroes, because they have no history or accomplishments.'"

Arturo frowned, furled his brow, and raised his voice. "That was so ridiculous and offensive! I was determined to write a report about a Negro who accomplished a lot. I thought of my mother and wanted to write about what a wonderful, intelligent woman she was, even though she didn't have much formal education. But then I thought my mother would be too humble of a person to win the respect of that terrible teacher. So, after some research, I decided to write about the achievements of Booker T. Washington, who was a child of slaves but found a way to get educated and became the first leader of Tuskegee University. I thought this was more of the report my teacher wanted." Arturo took a long, deep breath and added, "But she gave me a C-and put no comments in the margins."

We all grumbled.

"God bless you, though, for speaking up for our people," said Aaron Douglas.

One of the guild members said, "You are a fascinating man and so driven to bring respect to our race, but what has brought you to us in particular?"

Arturo said with great conviction, "I want to make people more aware of the contributions that Afro-Latins and Afro-Americans have made to American society. I want to collect and exhibit things like slave narratives, quilts, poems, whatever our people did well against all odds."

Afro-Americans—that was a new term for me. I kinda liked the ring of it. I knew Alain Locke would really like that moniker.

"I may also want to collect pictures of the artwork of Miss Savage's WPA students and put them into a collection. I was thinking that maybe the art and artifacts I collect can be displayed at your library on 135th St."

Librarian Anne Bennis was at the meeting and shook her head enthusiastically, "Oh, yes, I'll help make that happen. Another of our librarians, Ernestine Rose, is accumulating things like that for future generations."

Arturo kept coming to our meetings. One night he asked, "How do you think we can use new art to reflect the contributions that Afro-Americans are making to this society?"

We sat there thinking for a while. Then Charles Alston, who I finally convinced the WPA to hire as a teacher, spoke up. "Murals. We can do it through murals."

The room was quiet for a while.

I got excited. "You're right, Charles. The WPA eventually wants us to do works of art for civic centers. Murals that depict our people interacting equally with people of other races would be wonderful!"

Charles said, "I'll come up with some ideas."

In the meantime, the WPA money allocated for hiring additional teachers was sitting around doing nothing. I wrote letters to the president and Mrs. Roosevelt. I brought a delegation to our local alderman. As time went on, I could see people wincing when I went into their office. If they heard my voice on the other end of the line, a cheery hello on the phone would turn to a somber, "Oh, hi, how are you?"

But eventually my persistence paid off. Slowly but surely, I got some Negro teachers hired. We employed more and more students. We displayed our art at our workshops for all to come and see, and people came and viewed it. Our WPA Harlem Community Arts program was becoming a huge success!

All the while Charles Alston was thinking about where and how to create murals to honor our people. He came up with the idea of producing murals

188

to cheer the bleak walls of the Harlem Community Hospital, and I approved it enthusiastically.

Under Charles' supervision, seven artists made a series of sketches. One was entitled Magic in Medicine and depicted traditional African people with their natural healing remedies. A second showed Negro people working alongside Whites as doctors and nurses. A third showed Negro people at play. The hospital objected to four of their sketches saying they focused too much on "Negro" subject matter and "Negroes may not form the greater part of the Harlem community in years to come." The controversy was brought all the way to President Roosevelt. Eventually, all of the sketches were approved, but it was almost like tyranny to depict Negroes and Whites as equals.

This mural controversy showed that while there were no Jim Crow laws up North, the majority of Whites here still didn't respect us. I got angrier and angrier, as did the rest of us members of the Harlem Art Guild. We didn't want equality way off in the distant future. We wanted it now!

Langston Hughes regularly attended our Art Guild meetings, and he was frustrated, too. He hired as his secretary a woman who had radical ideas for creating change. Her name was Louise Patterson. She started coming to our meetings with Langston. After graduating from Berkeley in 1923 with a degree in economics, Louise taught at Hampton Institute in Virginia, which had a Negro student body but a predominantly White administration. She supported a student strike there and later went to New York to study at the New School for Social Research. Louise greatly admired the Soviet system of a classless society. Some of us teased her good-naturedly— calling her Madame Moscow. However, she was a very serious woman, and we found she couldn't take a joke.

Louise assembled a cast of 22 Negroes—including Langston Hughes—to act in a Soviet film about race relations and labor disputes in the American South. The actors got all the way to Russia only to find the Russians canceled the film at the last minute. They said it was due to lack of funds, but Louise thought they were afraid this would cause problems with the American government.

Langston said, "I was looking forward to this opportunity, because I felt the Soviets could make quality pictures about people of color that didn't reduce us to minstrels."

Members of the Artists Guild said we needed to go further than our goals could take us. So, we decided to found what we called The Vanguard group. While helping Negro artists gain attention, it would also be at "the vanguard" of new ideas for social change in America. Nevertheless, we continued to sponsor art exhibits by our Negro artists at schools and churches in Harlem. We featured Jacob Lawrence in one of them. Again, this was in defiance of the Harmon Foundation where people without any artistic background decided whose work should be exhibited.

Mary Brady got wind of what we were doing. Wanting to punish us, she gave an interview to the papers saying that the members of the Vanguard group were Communists.

In one of our Vanguard meetings, I warned the group, "We have to be careful. Remember how Garvey talked about Communism even though he didn't think it was the answer for us?"

Someone piped up, "Yeah, and remember how he served some jail time and then got deported? That know-it-all Hoover from the Bureau might persecute us if he thinks we're Communists."

Langston declared indignantly, "Just because we believe The United States could use some improvement doesn't mean we want to overthrow it."

Eventually, though, my worst fears came true. A few suspicious-looking people came to our large meetings and tried to blend in, but they had nothing to say about politics, social issues or art. They just nodded like they agreed with everything.

I telephoned Langston. "Did you notice those outsiders who sit by so quietly?"

Langston said, "I sure did. There's a word for them—snitches. Sometimes people call them G-men: government men who work for Hoover."

Nervously, I asked, "What's Hoover trying to gain by sending people to spy on us? Does he really think a small group of artists and writers could overthrow the government?"

Langston's usually quiet voice rose. "Hoover is a fanatic. I have heard that if he thinks someone is communist he will ruin them by smearing their good name."

"But how?"

"He will send people out to investigate that person and dig up something he or she might want to hide."

Such as?" I asked.

"Like being a homosexual. He's got something against homosexuals. I heard he says 'both communists and homosexuals are sneaky people who hide in dark corners doing bad things.'"

I thought Langston was a homosexual, but that didn't matter to me. "Maybe he's really a homosexual at heart but doesn't want to admit it," I said.

Langston laughed. "That's probably true."

"He's got a lot of nerve, judging others." I added pompously, "Well, I don't have anything to hide."

Langston responded, "We all have secrets."

Leave it to Langston to be dramatic, I thought. But then I remembered I did have something to hide. I had done something illegal, some would say immoral. I was a bigamist, since I did not get a divorce from James Savage when I married Robert Poston.

THIRTY

Something in me turned a corner—a dark one. I began seeing spies everywhere. At stores, I imagined people were looking at me funny. At the art center, if two people were talking in hushed tones, I thought they were talking about me. Then I feared my radio might have special powers to record what I was thinking. When that happened, I realized I was going over the edge.

One Sunday morning as I was sitting and thinking my odd thoughts, I heard a knock at the door.

"Please don't make it be a G-man," I prayed.

More knocking. I sat transfixed. Finally, I opened my door a crack...with the chain on it. It was only Irene. Praise the Lord! I was never so relieved to see her.

Before she hung up her coat, she said, "You don't look so good."

"I don't?" I hadn't looked in a mirror all weekend. Irene had been staying at her cousin's for a couple of days to watch her cousin's baby.

In that voice used by grown children who think they need to parent their parents, she said accusingly, "You've got dark circles under your eyes, and your hair looks like a bird's nest." Where was my little Irene who was once too afraid to question me?

She caught me at a weak moment when I couldn't give her a stinging retort. I simply said, "Oh, I didn't realize it, but I haven't gone out all weekend."

"Still..." she began firmly, like there wouldn't be any allowances made.

Irene turned on the radio. We sat on the couch.

I asked her how it went with the baby. She said "Fine," but she added, "I miss Grandma."

"Yeah, I miss her, too."

She stared at me for a few seconds and asked with real concern, "What are you doing with yourself —that's giving you dark circles?"

In a rare moment of sharing with my daughter and her actually listening, I told her about the things that bothered me lately—the discrimination by the WPA and J. Edgar Hoover's infiltration.

Irene said, "Now, I know why you have dark circles under your eyes. Is all this worth it— especially the Communism stuff? Maybe you should get out of that Vanguard Club."

I sighed, "Maybe you're right, Irene. I'd feel like a coward though." I went into the kitchen and brought back an apple for Irene and me. "Want one?" I asked.

Irene took it. As we munched together, I tossed around some ideas in my head. Between bites, I said, "You know, Irene, the one thing that matters to me most—besides you—is that I have helped with the education of 1,900 young people who are living their dream of becoming artists. If Hoover found a way to toss me in jail like he did with Garvey, I couldn't keep working for the WPA."

"You're absolutely right," Irene agreed.

One night after dinner when I was home alone, I heard another knock on the door. I was getting to hate those unexpected knocks. What could it be this time?

I called through the door, "Who is it?'

"It's Jonathon Powers," said a sweet, low, masculine voice.

"I don't know you. Go away."

"I am sorry to bother you, Miss Savage, but I have an important message." The voice was still sweet and low.

"About what?" I demanded.

"I am from the government and am hoping to have a word or two with you to keep you from disaster."

"Disaster? What disaster?" I couldn't hide the fright in my voice.

"If you have a lock with a chain, I could show you my identification card."

Reluctantly, I opened the door a few inches, just as far as the chain would allow.

And there on his ID card was his picture. Smiling, clean-shaven, white, with a shirt and tie. And part of Bureau of Investigation.

I said I didn't want to talk to him, but he insisted this would be for my good. Not talking to him would only bring me trouble, he said.

Very reluctantly, I let him in.

The man was tall, slender and full of charm. He made himself comfortable on my couch, even though I had not invited him to do so. I remained standing. He told me about the government's concern about our Vanguard Club. His eyes took in what he could see of my small apartment. In his syrupy sweet voice, he said, "I am sure you do not want to overthrow our government. Is that right?"

"Yes, that's right," I said sullenly.

"We could help you do a lot better in life, if you would just help us."

When I told him I didn't want to help, he said, "But there would be some good money in this for you. Maybe you could even get into a better apartment."

I thought I was used to living in the tenements, but my mind went quickly to a fancy apartment in Lower Manhattan. I fought that desire, though, and said, "I don't care what you're willing to give me."

"All we want is a little information. Not so much about what is said in the meetings, but about the personal lives of its members—if there are things certain individuals wouldn't want anyone to know. Like we are aware that Langston Hughes is homosexual, but are there any other homosexuals?

195

Has anyone been in a mental hospital or committed a crime?"

He stirred the savage in me. "Get out of my house, Mister, and never come back again!"

When he didn't stand up, I grabbed the hat he put on my couch and took it to the door with me, "Take your hat and go!"

Slowly, he stood. Slowly, he took back his hat. And, slowly, he said in a not-so-sweet voice, "You'll be sorry."

I was glad I stood up to Jonathan Powers, but now my mind became even more agitated. When he left, I thought about his threat, "You'll be sorry." Would he or one of his co-workers follow me, listen into my conversations, and, worst of all, do something bad to me or my daughter?

Again, I saw spies and enemies everywhere. I saw them in shadows, in alleys, in my apartment's hallway. They were furtive, darting figures that disappeared almost as soon as I saw them. This same young woman who took the train by herself from Florida to New York without knowing where she was going was now afraid of everything. The good thing was that I knew I was overreacting. That kept me sane. But the fear that someone was always out to get me was an unwelcome emotion—one that I was afraid I'd have to beat down for a long time.

As much as I wanted to brainstorm with my fellow Vanguard members to improve the situation for Negroes in America, I knew I couldn't do it any more. And so I went to the next meeting dreading what I felt called to say, "My dear friends, I regret that I will have to quit the Vanguard Club."

Everyone exclaimed at the same time, "What!"

I was honest with them about the visit from the G-man. So what if there were some infiltrators in the room? Let them tattle on me to J.Edgar Hoover.

t night wore on, I thought, On this
the only thing missing is the warm
oving man. However, I'd had such bad
that I put that thought out of my mind.
e next months, I continued to teach,
work on my statue. One afternoon as I
ing touches on *Realization*, I heard the
supervisors whispering behind my back.
orking with the Bureau of Investigation?
nfiltrating our workshop? Lately, there
lot of hushed whispering around the art
tever they were talking about brought
rs, and I couldn't push them away.

I left my apartment to go to work the next
hich happened to be Halloween,) I noticed
oing to school dressed as ghosts and
was a balmy day and the wind lifted pieces
, dry leaves and scraps of paper and set
irling around. The atmosphere heightened
Scurrying to work, I felt sure something bad
to happen.

hen I entered my office, and turned on the
ple jumped out at me. *Oh, no! My end has*

But they only yelled, "Surprise!"
almost fainted. They told me they had
d in the last month to gather money to have
lization sculpture cast in bronze. Teachers and
as well as their friends and relatives from
had chipped in. My mind flashed back to
Cove Springs, where people helped one
, like when my daddy's friends took us in
s to the train station.

One of my students gave a little speech. "This
ure speaks to us in Harlem. You are a sculptor
people, Miss Savage. You show the realization
ams deferred or forever lost because of the color
he's skin. We all hope for better for our
ation, but we know that our ancestors and many

He'd probably be thrilled to know he had frightened
this formerly brave woman.

After that, most of my peers from the
Vanguard group distanced themselves from me. That
was understandable, but I felt more alone than ever.

THIRTY-ONE

I decided to concentrate solely on my work and my teaching. I resolved to avoid any issues that could lead to confrontations.

I heard the clay call again. This time it said, *Feel me, mold me, shape me. I will heal you.*

The WPA had supplied our schools with an abundance of art supplies—including clay. However, fewer students were interested in sculpture than in the other art forms. Most of the clay went unused. So, in my spare time, I decided to heed the call of the clay and return to sculpting. I could use my work as a teaching tool for the few who liked to sculpt.

As always, it took me a while to come up with an idea. I finally decided to capture the moment when a Negro man and woman grasp that their future will only hold travail. A woman sits with a cloth covering her only from the waist down. A man crouches next to her looking lost and terrified. They are like one unit. I called the piece, *Realization*, but I never interpreted to anyone the time or place of this couple's distress. Little did anyone know how personal it was for me.

The piece was nearly life-sized. I worked on it in a corner of our gigantic workshop. As I sculpted, students and supervisors stopped to watch. They marveled at its sad beauty and even brought their friends and relatives to come look.

One day I finished work early and came home. I felt lighter than usual. I didn't see any spies or enemies, and I didn't worry about them hiding in the stairwells. Things were quiet in my life. I finally got Negro teachers hired. I collected a steady paycheck. I was done with the Vanguard group.

V
down, I l
were still
smudges. A
way out of
it.

On
painting give
I taught clas.
lovingly. I sta
sitting on a lor
One was of the
Another was or
memories of Da
pieces of mine
sculptures were l
time creating the
company. Sitting c
with the knowledg
former student, G
wall behind me. I fe

Although ou
in front and back, the
unusually fresh on this

For a change,
home from work, I
worked on a sculptin
meeting. But I just sat.
had helped several ye
artwork and had stayed
else.

I got the feeling a
the stairs might contain
sculptures I had molded.
asked myself. And even *Wh*
to feel good and not think too

I went into the kit
hocks and cabbage.

As tha
peaceful day
embrace of a l
luck with men
For th
supervise and
put the finish
students and
Were they w
Were spies i
had been a
center. Wha
back my fea
As
morning (w
children g
goblins. It
of rubbish
them to sy
my fears.
was going
V
light, pee
come!

conspire
my *Rea*
students
Harlem
Green
anothe
wagon

sculpt
of our
of dre
of o
gene

of our peers here in Harlem have felt like that man and woman."

Now when I came home I had not only a sense of peace, but also a feeling of elation. I kept saying to myself, *People appreciate my work, and finally one of my most important works will be cast in bronze.*

A kind supporter from Harlem came with his old truck to pick up my sculpture and take it to a nearby foundry. When they finished casting *Realization*, I went to look at it. I was so overcome with emotion that I shed a few tears. For advertising purposes, I had a photographer take a picture of me with my creation.

Although I knew I had probably burned my bridges with members of the Vanguard group, I called Anne Bennis and asked her if any of our old friends might have a connection with someone who would purchase the statue. I invited her to come over one night for a cup of tea and gave her the photograph that she could show. A couple weeks later, she reported back to me that everyone loved it, but didn't know anyone who might purchase it. I called the galleries, but they said they didn't have room for such a large piece.

However, I did get some good news from one of the places I called—The Architectural League in New York City. If I sent them a picture and they liked it; they would put it in their upcoming exhibit. Upon receiving the photo, they were impressed and agreed to show *Realization*. I was delighted when I won an Honorable Mention. The exhibition was not meant for selling art, but often people who view works of art at exhibitions offer to buy them. No one offered to buy *Realization*.

When would I ever learn that sculpting my Negro people would only lead to rejection? No matter how touching and beautiful my sculpture was no one wanted to face my Colored brother and sister at the realization of their unhappy destiny in life. America couldn't deal with that.

In my study of art history books at the 135th St. Library, I remembered looking at pictures of Michelangelo's marble creations of two Roman slaves. They were seven feet tall and were to be put on the tomb of the pope. True, they were supposed to represent some kind of allegory, but everyone approved of Michelangelo sculpting such sad slaves in marble! Why couldn't Americans look at my sad figures? Was it because they were Negro?

I got irritated with myself. Just when I had been feeling at peace and not getting my hopes up too high anymore, my peers at the WPA had given me new hope. However, again I realized that hopes for my artistic success were in vain.

When I personally had that "realization," I stared sadly into space like the forlorn subjects of my sculpture. But I wasn't just sad. I felt my savage side coming out. I didn't explode, but in the following days, I was "touchy" with supervisors and students at work. I growled at my secretary when she didn't have something typed as quickly as I wished.

Anne Bennis called me and told me she was going to a concert at Town Hall, a performance space in midtown Manhattan. Marian Anderson would be singing, and Anne wanted to come tell me about it afterwards. "Maybe it will get your mind off of that sculpture," she added.

"Maybe," I answered.

When Bennis arrived, she raved about Marian Anderson. "I was so impressed! To think that a Negro woman could reach the heights she has in America. I read somewhere that Marian had a very tough life as a child, but because she sought out voice training wherever she could and because she had such great talent, she became a star. Tonight, she sang everything from spirituals to opera. I was mesmerized."

My savage heart pounded with anger. I yelled at Anne. "I'm just as important, just as much an artist as Marian Anderson, and you don't rave about me!"

My friend looked at me like I was crazy. At the moment, I probably was.

Although I was in no the mood to be polite, I asked Anne if she wanted something to eat and drink. When she said she did, I banged the plates and cups so loudly in the kitchen that even my ears hurt. When Anne tried to make light conversation, I sulked. My rage festered.

Anne was too sweet of a person to talk back to me. In a fleeting moment, I thought, *I probably need someone like my father who could put me in my place or maybe Josephine Baker. She wouldn't tolerate me feeling sorry for myself.*

I started seeing spies again. Once when I left the Art Center I swore that the heels of a government man were clicking behind me. As the clicking got closer and closer, I walked up the steps of a brownstone building that was not where I lived. Without so much as a glance, the man with the clicking heels kept walking and never looked back. Another time when I went out the front door of the Center I felt sure I saw Joe Gould peaking around the corner. I walked over to yell at him, but no one was there.

Two weeks later I came home—still in a fuss. Irene was working the late shift at the laundry. It didn't help that I was alone. On this particular day, I heard news that one of my students had sold a decorative painting for a good amount. *Why won't anyone buy my sculpture?*

I began pacing around the apartment and yelling over and over, "Why not mine?"

I screamed. I took a knife from my kitchen drawer and went into the front room where my unsold sculptures stared at me. I felt like they were yelling, *Why not us? Why couldn't you sell us?* I wanted to shut them up. I lifted the knife above my head, but a still, small voice said, *No, don't do it Gussie! What's wrong with you?*

I lowered the knife, turned it over in my hand, and eventually dropped it to the floor.

Then I heard the handle of the door turning. Ooh, I forgot to attach the chain! It was only Irene. Thank God.

Breathing hard, I turned towards her.

She looked around and asked, "Mom! What's going on?"

She must have seen the madness in my eyes. Looking at the knife on the floor, she said in a shaky voice, "Here, Mom, come by me. Let's sit down."

I sat down with Irene but at the edge of the couch. With teeth chattering, I uttered, "All my work, sculpting our people, has led to nothing. No one cares about us. No one wants to look at us. I am so sick of it all!"

"What do you mean, 'no one cares about us'? I don't get it."

I told her my theory about *Realization*—about how it was one more example of how Whites and some Coloreds didn't want to buy the sculpture, because it reminded them of how we Negro people have suffered.

In a rare show of affection, Irene reached over and put her hand on mine.

She said, "I know how long and hard you worked on that statue. When I saw it at the exhibit, it moved me."

Irene offered further comfort. "Try not to worry yourself any more. At first, you made it for the students to learn from it at the Art Center anyhow, didn't you?"

I shook my head in agreement

"Return to that being your goal. Get it put back in the art center, and just try to relax."

I appreciated Irene's attempt to comfort me, but it was still difficult to pull myself back from the brink of despair... again. Nonetheless, I tried.

I reflected on those recent quiet, lovely afternoons at home. I tried to go back to that place.

Also, the students' interactions at the Art Center could be entertaining. So I attempted to enjoy that facet of my job. For instance, a budding romance at the center was fun to observe. Jacob Lawrence fell in love with my student from Barbados, Gwendolyn Knight. They got engaged. I asked Gwendolyn to sit for an hour a day while I sculpted her face. She loved how it turned out, and I gave it to her as a wedding present. Jacob and Gwendolyn seemed to be a perfect couple.

My savage heart gradually began to heal again. I turned to the clay once more. I got an inspiration. I would hold out no hope for my piece to be purchased, but I wanted to create.

My sculpture had to do with war. Rumblings were sounding in Europe about the possibility of another conflict. The recent world-wide war in which my brother served left a sad imprint on me; I didn't want to see so many lives lost again. I would call my piece, *After The Glory*. I would sculpt (two-thirds life sized) a Negro grandmother, a daughter and her child gazing into space looking for their missing men

I remembered Francisco Goya's painting, *The Third of May 1808* in which Goya painted a terrified-looking Spanish citizen with his arms extended widely in the moment before a French soldier killed him in a firing squad. Goya used art for political reasons—to make people see up close and personal the horrors of war. Just recently Pablo Picasso did a giant mural called *Guernica* that was lauded as a moving and powerful anti-war painting. I too wanted to make my statement about the devastation wrought by war...even though the statement was only for me and my students.

205

As I worked, my students and the teachers admired it like they did *Realization*. I told them this time to please not collect any money to have it cast in bronze. My piece would be a great addition to a park with a memorial space for veterans or could go into a museum, but I knew that in the 1930s, the Big Shots with the money didn't care how a war might affect the people I sculpted—Negroes.

To those who admired the piece while I sculpted, I said, "I'm just doing it because I have to sculpt and want to express something I think is important. I'm doing it for me... and for teaching purposes here."

I met with the sculpture teachers and told them, "Please feel free to use *After The Glory* and *Realization* to teach students how to sculpt people in all different positions. However, I want you to warn your students: depicting our people when they suffer probably won't make a penny in sales. Abstracted African masks or nostalgic paintings of Negro gatherings might sell but not our Negroes if they showed any hint of frustration."

THIRTY-TWO

People said Joe Gould kept asking about me. He got a job with the Federal Writers project (part of the WPA), which I hoped would keep him busy. I was glad he wasn't making any unexpected appearances lately, although sometimes I still feared he would jump out from behind a tree or wall

In the meantime, trouble started brewing for the Harlem Community Art Center as a whole. Our local congressman called me and said, "Word is that Southern politicians demand of Franklin Roosevelt that he reduce funding for the national arts program. They said it costs the country too much money and that we are coming out of The Depression anyhow so maybe there will be more jobs soon."

I was shocked. "That's terrible," I moaned. It took a moment for this to sink in. Then I asked, "Are they thinking about cutting any other programs?"

He answered, "You're not going to like this, but actually, they didn't complain about the WPA employees who build bridges and schools. They seem to see the art programs with actors, dancers, artists and writers as unnecessary luxuries in the grand scheme of things."

"Wouldn't you know it?" I mused more to myself than the congressman. "Is there anything I can do?"

"I'm sorry, Miss Savage. I anticipate they won't cut all of your people, but they may cut some. You do employ a lot."

"Hmph. We're being punished because I've made the art program into such a success." However, I knew the congressman was not to be blamed.

He got quiet, then added, "Some of those Southerners have heard that you artists are a bunch of communists."

I was tired of that old allegation. I addressed what I thought was the real issue: "Oh, and did they have the guts to admit they wanted to cut the program because most of our participants are Negro?"

"Miss Savage, must you always be so abrasive?"

The man was speaking from experience with me. I had talked with him several times before about the need for the WPA to hire more Negro supervisors for my program, and he tried to make my case heard whenever he could. In a calmer tone, I said, "You know I've complained a lot to you and other politicians about the injustices. You've been the only one to really listen, and I appreciate it. Are you sure there's nothing I can do or say about this?"

"Don't feel you have to kill yourself on this one. It's being handled in Washington D.C., not New York City. Just keep doing the excellent job you're doing. Nothing too extreme will happen in the immediate future."

I sighed. "Thanks for letting me know."

I realized that eventually the WPA programs would all have to come to a halt if our economy improved. It was good that more people were getting jobs, but why did our art center in Harlem have to be the first to go or be reduced?

Thank goodness that something fantastic happened to get my mind off this.

One of the happiest days of my life occurred when I came home from work, hung up my coat, and went to change clothes. The phone rang, and a man with a low, gravelly voice said . "Hello, Miss Savage. You have been selected to do a large sculpture for the 1939 World's Fair." I thought I died and went to heaven

The man from the planning committee requested that my sculpture represent the American Negro's contribution to music, especially song. The committee would pay for all my expenses along with a monetary commission. A few other female artists were also commissioned to do sculptures.

I called Irene at work. Word eventually spread to people who had come to discussions at my apartment—Langston Hughes, Countee Cullen, Aaron Douglas, Zora Neale Hurston, Gwendolyn Bennett, etc. Even though they were probably still angry with me for quitting the Vanguard Club, some of them called to congratulate me.

Seeing as how it would take two years to create the statue, there was one problem, and it was a big one. I would have to quit my job at the Harlem Community Art Center. That job was what I lived for. I thought and thought about it, and then I came up with the idea of asking for a leave of absence. When I brought this up to the WPA administrators, they were more than happy to give me the leave and to "temporarily" give my job to my supposed friend and co-worker, Gwendolyn Bennett.

Luckily, I knew another Negro artist, Louise Jefferson, who had a home studio and a big enough backyard for my World's Fair statue. She kindly let me use her interior and exterior spaces.

The nice part about this commission was that I got paid to think. After a couple of weeks of thought, I knew I wanted my work to reflect the Negro spirituals and hymns I learned as a child. I decided to use as inspiration the song that James Weldon Johnson had written. It was called, "Lift Every Voice and Sing," and it became our Negro national anthem. Thoughts returned to me of how we sang it at school every morning after saying the Lord's Prayer. The song was full of hope, because it was written soon after our parents were freed from slavery. Little did any of us realize how long it would take for us to really savor the liberties we dreamed of. However, I still loved this song, and I especially remembered its first verse —

Sing a song full of the hope that the present has brought us

Lift every voice and sing, till earth and Heaven ring,
Ring with the harmonies of liberty;
Let our rejoicing rise, high as the listening skies,
Let it resound loud as the rolling sea.
Sing a song full of the faith that the dark past has taught us,
Facing the rising sun of our new day begun,
Let us march on till victory is won.

The lyrics had special significance for me, because I knew James Weldon Johnson so well. When I called James and told him about my decision to use his song as inspiration, he said, "That's great, Augusta, but you're going to have some kind of challenge figuring out how to put my song into clay. A song isn't something you see."I laughed and said, "I do have my work cut out for me."

For two more weeks, I rummaged through my mind for a plan, and then it came! I saw my finished project as clear as day. It would be a huge harp—going up to sixteen feet tall. The strings would be a line of singing Negro children. The base of the harp would consist of a gigantic arm and hand with the fingers curving upward, symbolizing God's hand. In the foreground a kneeling young Negro man would offer a plaque with musical notes to represent the musical gifts of Negro people.

I wanted each of my twelve harp strings to have a face of a different child. So, I needed to recruit twelve children to be models. I figured I would sit on the steps of Louise's house to recruit them. However, people in this part of Harlem didn't know me, and they might think I was absconding with their children.

So, I talked Louise into sitting with me and encouraging neighbors to let their children pose. All I asked of each child was for him or her to sit for 15 minutes while I sketched. I paid each 15 cents for the work. Some could sit still and were fine models; others couldn't, and I had to let them go.

Then I needed to find a boy turning into a man—young and a perfect example of God's creation of humanity. I didn't realize how difficult it would be. Many candidates didn't notice me staring at them as they walked down the street, but some did.

"Whatcha lookin' at, Lady?" said one, as he glared at me.

Finally, I found Gordon—hopefully the perfect fellow. Of course, I had to explain what I was doing, "Young man, I am doing a sculpture for the upcoming World's Fair. Perhaps, I'd like you to be in it, if you'd consider it."

Looking bewildered, he could only ask, "What?" My first impression was that Gordon seemed shy and serious. Just the kind of person I was looking for. He crinkled up his face as if he wondered whether he could trust me. Finally he said, "I'm on my way to work, but I could stop by tomorrow...maybe a little earlier than this."

The next morning at 6:45 a.m., I sat on the steps waiting for Gordon, and there he came walking down the sidewalk...slowly and hesitantly.

I got up and walked over to him. "Hello. So glad you came back. I failed to introduce myself yesterday. I am Augusta Savage. I run the Harlem Community Art Center."

Gordon's face broke into a smile. "Oh, I've heard of you."

I felt myself glowing. "I'm the one."

After explaining the project, I asked him to come by after his job so I could show him the beginning of my sculpture in the backyard. When Gordon showed up, I told him about the unique pose he would need to assume, if he were willing. He was, and I had him pose several times. Oh, the patience and leg strength Gordon exhibited to squat and lean forward holding the plaque for all to see! I paid him a whole $5.00, but there really wasn't enough money in the world to pay him for making my imagined statue into an eye-catching reality.

Late one afternoon when I came home, I sat in my living room without going to my kitchen or sculpting table. I was in that quiet, peaceful space again. I reflected. By now I was into my mid-forties. Josephine Baker had predicted that by this time I would have accomplished a lot. This sculpture was my last big chance. I'd better make it count.

It took two full years to complete. When it was just about finished, James Weldon Johnson came over to visit me at Louise's. I took him outside for a viewing.

Wordlessly, he walked around my massive creation, looking at the figures from every angle. Finally, James gave me a big smile. "My, my, Augusta. I never thought you could translate a song into a sculpture, but you did!"

"I have Louise to thank for letting me use her space, but I'm delighted that you like it."

"I certainly do. Your larger children composing the harp are quite tall. Did you need a ladder to work on them?"

"Oh, yes."

In disbelief, he said, "This is so enormous. Don't your arms get tired?"

"Yep."

"I hope you don't mind me saying so, but you're such a slender, elegant woman. I'm just amazed that you could do this...." His voice trailed off.

I laughed. "My arms are as strong as a dock worker's."

"I guess so." He turned from gazing at the sculpture and looked at me with utmost sincerity. "I just wanted to thank you for choosing my song as the theme, especially since it's such an old song—around for thirty years or so now."

I said with certainty, "It's a great song. Although you wrote it for our people, it can speak to anyone who is hoping for a better future."

James nodded in agreement. "True," he said. Then he gave me a brief hug. After he said goodbye, James walked towards his car with a bounce to his step that I had never seen before.

Of course, I loved the act of creating, but being paid well for my sculpting was a much-needed bonus. Halfway through my work, the World's Fair Commission made me a consultant to the project at $1,800 a month, and a few months later a project supervisor at $1,750 yearly. Now that I was financially secure and not currently threatened by any G-men or Joe Gould, I felt free of worry.

Every couple of weeks I stopped by the Art Center to see how things were going. After all, this was my regular job and I wanted to make sure that all was running well. I'd chat with Gwendolyn Bennett, and she'd assure me that the center was in good hands until I returned.

One evening at Louise's backyard, I finally put the finishing touches on *Lift Every Voice and Sing,* and I walked around it to judge the results. "I did it! I did it!" I screamed and ran inside to crow to Louise.

She asked, "What?"

"I finished my sculpture, and it's beautiful!" I screamed again.

We joined hands and jumped up and down like little kids. Louise said, "Let's uncork some wine and celebrate."

During the next few days, I carefully covered my massive statue with a substance that made it look like black basalt. Finally, the time came for it to be installed outside at the Fair.

Movers came and carefully loaded my piece into their truck. After seeing them off, I took a subway and a bus to the fairgrounds. As I traveled, I thought about how different it was with my statues *Realization* and *After the Glory*. I said to myself, *This is the way it should be when you create a great work of art. It is actually installed at a prominent place where people can view it and contemplate its meaning.*

The fair was spread out over acres of land in Flushing-Meadows, a vast open area in Queens, NYC. My statue would be in the court of The Contemporary Arts Building. I had viewed and studied the site already a few times. Now I watched the workers dig a gigantic hole so the statue could be lowered into it. They covered its base with dirt, and they worked until it was firmly planted.

When I went to bed that night, I pondered that the creation and installation went perfectly. Now the challenging part would follow: watching the reactions of the mostly White spectators.

On opening day, I went to the site. *Now I'll see what I'm up against.* The first family to come by was composed of a White father, mother and two elementary-school-age children.

They smiled, and the father said to me, "Are you the sculptor?"

"Yes." My voice shook slightly.

"This is really beautiful," he said, and his wife and children nodded in agreement.

When I replied, "Thank you," they would never know how thankful I was. All day long and into the coming weeks and months, people—almost all being White—made nothing but complimentary remarks.

I called James Johnson and told him how positive the reception was. I added, "You know, I hadn't thought about it, but this may be the first time many of these Whites have seen Negroes close-up. Viewing us in a work of art lets them study us without appearing rude."

James answered, "You make a good point. Also, think about the kind of people who come to a World's Fair. The fair is all about innovative ideas for the future. These are intelligent, open-minded people who are looking for new ways of doing and thinking about things."

Out of the four sculptures by us women, mine was the most popular. Postcards were printed with my creation on them. Also, small replicas were made and sold in the souvenir shop.

Grover Whalen, organizer of the World's Fair, came by and asked me to pose the next week in a picture with him and one of the replicas. The picture would appear in the newspapers. For the photo, I picked out my prettiest dress and had Irene fix my hair.

When I saw our picture in the paper, I bought five copies and came running home with them. "Look, Irene, I'm a celebrity!"

My daughter laughed as she responded, "And me, your talented hairdresser, deserves all the credit for making you look so beautiful!"

Hope started springing up in me again. I just turned forty-eight, but finally perhaps I was rising from the clay pit to a world stage of prominence.

I realized another thing. No middleman or woman had to be involved with my World's Fair sculpture: no gallery, no Harmon Foundation, no agent. My work went directly to the people, and they liked it! As always, when I could connect directly with people—Negro or White—they liked my art. *But how often will this happen in the future?* I asked myself. *How often will I be invited to do something like this to get my artwork out in front of the people without a middleman?*

I could have been devastated when one art critic reviewed my creation and said, "It is a superficial combination of fantasy and realism and is poorly composed." The critic was probably one of those high and mighty ones who saw me as a low class troublemaker still living in Harlem. I don't know how many people read the review, but crowds still came by and admired my work.

THIRTY-THREE

At my apartment one day I received a fancy looking letter with the words Works Progress Administration embossed on the envelope's return address. I hardly ever received mail from the WPA. *This has to be big*, I thought. And I was right. I tore open the envelope and read that since I was now gainfully employed as a sculptor, I was no longer eligible to continue as director of the arts center. The letter went on to say that the whole reason for the WPA was to get people employed, and now I—for one—was employed. My ire grew with each word, and it became intolerable when I read the following words: "Gwendolyn Bennett will permanently take over your position."

I immediately called Gwendolyn at home. It was about eight o'clock in the evening.

When I told her about the letter, she said, "Oh, that's a shame. I didn't know…" She couldn't go on. Her protest was so lame I knew she was in on the whole thing. I slammed the phone onto its cradle.

This time my savage heart exploded in a massive way! I swore and swore. "I hate you, Gwendolyn Bennett. I hate you! You are my Judas— you betrayed me!"

I took all the tools out of my kitchen drawer and threw them one by one with all my might onto the floor. Then I stopped. I said to myself, *I don't want to destroy my property because of someone else. I want to destroy that someone else.*

I got my big purse and ran outside. It was a chilly, windy November night. It began to rain, but I didn't care. I caught a bus. I wanted to use every word or weapon I could to cut Gwendolyn Bennett to shreds.

As I sat seething, an elderly Negro lady sat next to me. Hearing me breathing hard and feeling me rock back and forth, she eventually said, "Honey, whatever is bothering you, maybe I can help."

I turned my head towards her and gave her a steel-cold look. She pulled back and didn't say another word. Yet she didn't move to another seat even when the bus emptied out. Somehow her reaction and her presence interrupted me. I seethed less. When the bus came to the stop near Gwendolyn's place, I hesitated. I didn't get up. I didn't get off.

Later as the old lady slowly rose to go, she said, "Goodbye and good luck."

I stayed on as the bus went full circle, getting off where I had begun the trip. A loud crack of lightning lit up the sky. According to my mother's radio horror stories, it was a great night for a murder, but not one by me.

Irene was out late with a new boyfriend. I burrowed into my bed and went into my "nothing state." Early the next morning I called Anne Bennis. She was always an objective soul. Groggily, she answered the phone, "What is it, Augusta, so early on a Saturday morning?"

I told her how I lost my job. She came to life. "What…what happened? That's awful!"

Choking back tears, I demanded, "How could they do that to me?

"Maybe there was no big plot against you. Maybe you shouldn't take it personally. Maybe it was just like the letter said about you being employed now."

"No! No!" I yelled. "There's more to it than that.

Anne implored me, "Please, not quite so loud. I haven't had my first cup of coffee."

As upset as I was at the moment, I admired Anne for finally giving me a little push-back. That was never easy for her

She continued, "Anyhow, if there was a plot against you, maybe it could be something else. Let me think. We know you started that wonderful art program and inspired so many young artists. You worked day and night there. Could it be that they wanted someone who wouldn't demand..."

"Demand!" I flew into a rage again. "I just asked that my opinions on hiring be honored and that White people—especially those with no background in art—shouldn't decide who's a good art teacher!"

Sweet Anne tried to settle me down. "I know, I know. And you were right, but people like Mary Brady probably didn't like that..."

I interrupted again. I had a revelation. "You know how Gwendolyn Bennett is. You've been with us in those poetry and Vanguard meetings. She butters up people if she thinks it will be to her advantage."

Anne considered that. "So, maybe they wanted Bennett in because she wouldn't rock the boat?"

I said, "Exactly. She was probably happy to accept the traitor money anyhow, since she doesn't make much money for her poetry...even though I gotta admit it's good."

We both quietly mulled things over through the phone lines.

Then I mused, "But she worked with us in The Vanguard Club. I'm surprised they don't worry that she's a Communist."

Anne replied, "For all the time you worked for the Art Center they never brought up the Communist stuff against you."

I said, "Yes, but I was the only person with a successful art center already up and going. The WPA probably didn't think they had any choice but to have me."

"So true. The kids and grownups in Harlem love you. The Big Shots were probably afraid students wouldn't sign up if it wasn't for you."

My blood quit boiling so much. "Anyhow, I was told by our Congressman that they're going to slowly quit funding the Art Center, because the Depression is winding down, and art will be the first thing to go."

"So, you'd be out of a job eventually anyhow?" Anne asked in a reassuring tone.

"I guess so. I just wish it didn't have to end like this. Thanks for listening, Anne. You've always been there for me."

She laughed, "Even though I praised Marian Anderson?"

"I must admit I was a bit of a crab that night." I laughed, too, and we hung up.

It helped a lot to share my thoughts with Anne. Sitting on my couch with those remaining shards of my destroyed sculptures, I realized that too many times I handled my problems on my own. In this situation, I was lucky that the unknown lady on the bus broke my spell and that my friend Anne helped me to stay calm.

I once heard that the most important thing we possess is "our name." If we destroy our good name through an especially evil deed, people will not remember us well no matter what we have accomplished. I came so close to losing my good name. I don't know what I would have done if I made it to Gwendolyn's apartment. That not knowing concerned me.

I knew I had a problem. I needed to control my savage heart. But how?

As usual, after I got back to normal, it was uncomfortable to think about my reckless behavior. I was like a drunk who, after the hangover wears off, pretends like it never happened.

It was easier to put my energies into being at the fair every day. I loved chatting with the spectators who over and over told me how much they loved my work. Yet, I couldn't quit thinking about the sudden loss of my role at the Arts Center. Already, I missed the students and teachers. My pride wouldn't let me set foot in that place again.

Irene was in and out of the apartment, and so I tried to keep myself together for her. However, when she went to work, I took to my bed and let myself sink into my "nothing state."

To relax, I went back to spending time at the 135th St. Library—always my home away from home. One day I re-read a letter from my favorite librarian, Sadie Peterson, who had gotten me the commission to do the DuBois bust. A few years after she organized our poetry group, she left to run a library for the Veterans Administration in Tuskegee, Alabama.

I often looked back at her letter for inspiration:

Dear Augusta,

I hope you are doing well, and I hope that the librarians who followed me at the 135th St. Library have kept up our wonderful collection of Negro books and poems.

When I came to the VA, they hardly had any books. There are so many men who were injured in the war, and so many old men left here at the VA to die alone.

I have greatly enlarged our library collection. I ask each man what he likes to read, and then I make sure I get books and magazines that appeal to him. I believe in bibliotherapy—the treatment of patients through selected reading. You may remember that I was a social worker before I became a librarian.

What we do for others is the most important thing in life, isn't it?

Enough about me. I hope you are doing well. I often think of your perfect busts of Marcus Garvey and W.E.B. DuBois.

Sincerely,
Sadie Peterson

In this time of crisis, I focused on Sadie's words, "What we do for others is the most important thing in life." It gave me comfort to think about how I had helped so many young people find their way as artists—even if I never got a chance to say goodbye.

Librarians remained my favorite people, and I guess they liked me, too. The latest librarian at the 135th St. Library surprised me with a welcomed request. She said the Friends of the Library had collected money for me to do a bust of James Weldon Johnson.

"We in Harlem consider him to be one of our greatest heroes. We're aware that you know him personally and you created that wonderful sculpture about his song. So, we thought you would be the ideal person to capture his character."

Music to my ears!

I had James come to my apartment every Tuesday evening, and I also invited his wife, Grace Nail. I didn't want Grace thinking something was going on between me and her husband. Grace Nail's father was one of the people who sponsored me for the Rosenfeld scholarship to Paris. I felt deeply indebted to her and her family—people who believed in me. However, Grace soon quit coming. I was probably foolish to think she would be jealous. It took about ten sittings to capture James in clay.

Sitting and conversing with him was like working with Garvey and DuBois. I felt like I was in the presence of greatness. But, unlike Garvey and DuBois, James was relaxed. He wasn't a man of strong intellectual theories. He was more of a realist who took action as needed to clear up injustices. James held office in the NAACP and told me how he worked to get rid of things like poll taxes and literacy tests that would discourage Negroes from voting.

One evening James came into my apartment in a way that was totally unlike him. He threw down his coat, swore, and looked like he was on the verge of a savage heart attack. Immediately, I sensed his anguish.

"They lynched a man down South three days ago."

I winced. "I had hoped that was a thing of the past."

"I saw a picture in the paper of a Negro brother who was lynched by a crowd, because supposedly he had sworn at a White man who made a crude remark to his wife."

Shocked, I slammed down my sculpting tool. "That makes my blood boil!"

"You can believe I'll write a story about it for one of those newspapers I work for."

"Thank God we have you."

Fussing and fuming, I made a cup of tea for James; it took him a while to calm down enough to pose. And it took me a while to calm down enough to sculpt.

"Perhaps this isn't a good time for the sitting," I said gently.

"No, no, we must go on!" James said forcefully, like he was talking to himself as much as me.

That day as I sculpted his face, I added a new wrinkle of anger and a furrow of grief that had not been there before.

Two weeks later when I finally finished, I invited James and his wife Grace to view the bust together. Grace commented, "It looks just like my James," and James said, "I think you caught my soul." I was glad that I still had that gift.

Of course, the library paid for the sculpture and wanted to display it. Since there was no money for bronzing, I used my special mix that included brown shoe polish to give it a bronzy look.

Two weeks later, I received a call from Anne Bennis. The second I answered Anne said, "James Weldon Johnson has died."

"You just took a knife and stabbed my heart!" I cried.

"I'm sorry to be so blunt. I should have led up to it."

What happened?"

"He and Grace were taking a car trip in Maine. Grace was driving. A train hit their car. Thankfully, Grace survived."

I attended the funeral, as did 2,000 others. I hoped not to come in close contact with Gwendolyn Bennett. Otherwise, it was nice to see Langston Hughes, W. E.B. DuBois, Countee Cullen, Gwendolyn Knight, Zora Neale Hurston and all the others. I was disturbed, though, because I literally bumped into Joe Gould. He probably engineered it that way.

"It's so nice to see you again, Augusta," said Joe. By now, he was a waif of a man with dirty hair and smelly clothes. His bird nest of a beard bobbed up and down as he said, "I hope we can get together one of these days."

"Over my dead body," I fumed.

"I know where Irene works. Maybe I should pay her a visit and see if she can fix us up."

As slender and small as I was, I grabbed Joe's arm, faced him squarely, and said, "You visit her, and you will be dead meat."

"You're hurting me," he moaned.

"I'll hurt you more, if you ever go near her. Understand?"

I didn't let go of his arm until he said, "I understand."

224

Joe Gould scurried away like a mouse frightened by a kitten, but his odor remained.

THIRTY-FOUR

A couple of months later, the World's Fair was over. I couldn't make myself go on the day they bulldozed my sculpture. I wasn't the only artist who suffered. The sculptures of the other three female artists got bulldozed, too. I wished someone had come forward to cast mine in bronze. However, I was used to my best work being knocked down by mortality's iron fist.

I buoyed myself up by thinking about all of the spectators' praise and how they looked at my Negro subjects in the Harp with such respect. I remembered saying to myself, *This is your last big chance!* I took it and ran with it, and I succeeded in doing the best work of my life!

With the money I saved from the Fair, I could take time to decide what to do next. My two-year successful run gave me new energy. I would continue sculpting, but I would try some new angles to sell my art.

As a start, I made arrangements with the Argent Gallery to put on a one-woman show. The owner was happy to have me back.

The gallery had a small opening night for my show. Wearing a new dress and an imitation pearl necklace, I talked comfortably with the attendees. I exhibited my small. fanciful pieces from Paris and my two *Dahomean Women*. I put out my *Gamin* sculpture, but we enclosed it in glass and charged a pretty high amount for it (I really didn't want to let it go). Two of my best works, and *After The Glory*, sat in the back of the WPA warehouse or could have been thrown into the dump for all I knew. I still would not return to the art center. It was a shame that I couldn't display those sculptures. Many of my other best busts of famous people—were in their subjects' possession.

Someone did purchase one of my *Dahomean Women*, and that made me feel good. However, I got stinging reviews. Why, I don't know. My show ended quickly.

When the gallery called me and told me the news, I was listening to the fight between Joe Louis and John Henry Lewis. In the very first round, John was knocked down, and he was "out." I would not be like John. I was down, but I refused to be "out." There was still something in me that fought to succeed.

I decided to use what was left of my income from the fair to open my own gallery. In it, I would exhibit the latest and best work of my students and friends. I called it The Salon of Contemporary Negro Art. This was a big deal. As far as I knew, it was the first salon ever devoted exclusively to Negro art. Since I was the artist of my people in Harlem, I chose a location in the heart of Harlem. I couldn't afford anything in a fancier neighborhood anyhow.

I enjoyed the process of displaying the pieces to show them off in the best possible way. That was definitely a curator's job, but after arranging my students' works at the Art Center so many times, I was good at it.

By now, I had also learned how to plan an "opening." I made mine a black tie event, and I sent out 500 invitations to some of the most well known people in New York City. After all, I was semi-famous. Probably the poorest famous person in the world. But I did have my savings from the Fair to get this project going.

I wore a tasteful, but low-cut evening gown with an oversized bow, and my daughter gave me a corsage. I even had my hair done at a beauty shop. All evening, everyone complimented me on my looks. One of the White big businessmen whom I invited put his arm around me and whispered into my ear, "You look elegant tonight, Augusta." His remark was not unwelcomed.

People streamed in continuously. Countee Cullen hugged me and said my Salon was "gorgeous." Composer W. C. Handy attended, as well as writer Max Eastman and other prominent New Yorkers—both Negro andWhite.

My former student, Gwendolyn Knight, who had a piece in the show said, "I'm so nervous. I hope people like my work, but thanks so much for having me."

My writer friend, Zora Neale Hurston, commented, "Exquisite."

Millen Brand and his wife said, "Astounding."

Somehow Joe Gould heard about the opening and made an appearance. Looking wretched but still beaming with confidence, he cornered me. "You look ravishing." I turned on my heels and walked away.

I exhibited works by some of the biggest names in the Negro art world: Norman Lewis, Beauford Delaney, Elba Lightfoot, Ernest Crichlow and Gwendolyn Knight, to name a few.

By the time it was 11 p.m., only a few stragglers remained. Everyone had been in high spirits, admired the pieces and enjoyed the show. Countee and Langston had escorted out Joe Gould shortly after the opening began. The man was so drunk that he hardly resisted.

Anne Bennis and my daughter remained, helping me sweep the floor and straighten up.

"It was a great success, wasn't it?" Anne said. Irene echoed her sentiments.

My tone was far less enthusiastic. "Yes, it was, but did you notice I went to the money box only two times?"

"Darn it," said Irene. Anne just shook her head.

Within three months, I had to shut down my gallery. I hated having to call the artists to ask them to come back for their works. Defeat was a bitter pill to swallow.

Although it wasn't the nicest thought, I comforted myself with this: *At least I'm not the only Negro who can't sell her art.* Another thing that comforted me was that I was indeed the first person to open an art gallery with the expressed purpose of showcasing Negro art.

In spite of this setback, I persisted. I guess it was because of the many compliments the people at the Fair had showered on me. After a few weeks of mulling things over, I decided that besides trying new angles to sell my art, I would launch a new mission: to bring Negro art to people across the country. I called two newspapers and read them a prepared statement: *Our painting and sculpture, unlike our literature and music, has too long been the property of New York. I feel it is time for the rest of the country to know what the artists of our race are achieving.*

I decided to start with the Midwest. The Architectural League of Washington sponsored me to do a nine-city Midwestern tour concluding with the American Negro Exposition in Chicago.

Early in May I went to Chicago to set up an exhibition in Perrin Hall, adjacent to the Chicago Auditorium Theatre. People who attended my exhibition were allowed to purchase anything they saw. I brought two of my favorite works: *Gamin* and my bust of James Weldon Johnson (on loan from the library). Also, I brought my remaining *Dahomean Woman* and some small works from other Negro artists. The Architectural League of New York City did me a big favor. They went to the WPA warehouse, picked up *Realization* and sent it via railcar to the Auditorium Theatre. When I saw *Realization* again, it was like meeting up with a lost friend.

On a windy Chicago evening, a man held a gigantic door open for me as I entered the Chicago Auditorium Recital Hall. I was to make a speech to hundreds of prominent Chicago socialites. Nervous and excited, I looked out at the elegantly dressed audience. Edward H. Embree, head of the Rosenwald Fund, introduced me.

In a strong, dramatic voice, he said, "I have the pleasure of welcoming Augusta Savage, an artist who came from the humblest of beginnings to create beautiful sculpture. She is the first nationally known artist to depict the physical characteristics of Negro people. In the past, if Negroes were depicted at all, they were in the background, part of a larger work of art having to do with Whites. In addition, Augusta Savage has recruited and trained young people from the streets of Harlem to become some of the most important artists of our time. Tonight she is kind enough to show and tell us what the people of her race are creating. And so I present to you, Augusta Savage, artist of the people!"

Everyone clapped wholeheartedly.

I began, "Yes, I have brought many artists out of the impoverished streets of Harlem. Now they are famous, but many are still impoverished." I smiled to keep the mood light even though I was drawing attention to a harsh reality. "You've heard of 'the starving artist.' That's what many of us are, but we love what we do and wouldn't do anything else."

The auditorium was silent as each person looked at me intently and with an encouraging smile. The title of my talk was "Crisis: Past and Present." I started with telling my personal history and the three beatings a week from my father who did not understand an artist's instincts. I made a joke about it as I said with a laugh, "'He almost whipped all the art out of me." I progressed to how I went to Cooper Union and was discriminated against by the Fontainebleau Committee but eventually received another scholarship to Paris from the Rosenwald Foundation, our kind host of the evening. I told them about my teaching at the WPA Art Center and my sculpture at the World's Fair. People in the audience looked impressed that I had overcome and accomplished so much. In telling my story, I felt rather impressed myself.

But then I said what I really wanted to convey. "My greatest hope is that people will become more art conscious—that they will value the contribution of our Negro as well as our White artists to the beauty of the world and they will show this by purchasing our work."

Up until this point, I had the audience in the palm of my hand, but when I talked about people buying our art, I felt them pull away. They played with their purses and quit smiling.

Over light refreshments, I mingled genially with everyone. Individuals looked at, touched, and praised the sculptures I had on display. Many praised my speech and accomplishments. How this used to make my heart skip a beat! But I wasn't a timid child anymore who needed reassurance. I had all the confidence in the world in my work and that of my peers. Because no one bought our art that night, the compliments left me cold.

Yet, I didn't have time to sulk. I had made a commitment to run a three-day exhibition at the Chicago Southside YWCA, a powerhouse of an organization where I gave three talks a day to school children. *The Chicago Herald-American* newspaper reported that thousands of Negro students from Chicago schools came to hear me and see the art. I loved communicating with the children. Seeing me— a Negro woman—talking with them about art and looking successful seemed to inspire them. They were so innocent; I chose not to share all the heartaches accompanied by my supposed success. Let them be hopeful!

Seeing as how I didn't have the money to afford a hotel room and didn't know what hotels might accept a Negro, the plan was for me to reside at the homes of my Colored brethren. The first family was the Jones family—a Negro policeman, his teacher wife and their two small children. I noticed they had very little artwork on their walls. A piece in the kitchen was a still life of fruits in a bowl. A picture in the living room featured a neoclassical landscape with two White people in the foreground. Both were probably cheap reproductions bought at a place like Woolworth's Five and Dime. I knew that Woolworth's wasn't going to stock art by Negroes, but I asked myself again, *How are we Negro artists to support ourselves if our art isn't available and affordable for our own people?*

Thinking about these things while going to my host family's kitchen for a glass of water, I felt my body tighten. I was used to living alone where I could vent my frustrations, but I smiled sweetly to the couple and said I was going to retire to my room for the evening. Just as I sat down on my bed, I heard a phone ring.

Mrs. Jones called, "The phone is for you, Miss Savage!"

It was Anne Bennis. Immediately, I asked her, "Is there something wrong? Is Irene okay?"

"No, it's not bad news. I didn't think this family would mind if you got a call. I'm charged for it anyhow."

"So, what's happening?" I asked more casually as I sat on a stuffed chair next to the end table with the phone.

"I just wanted to catch you up on all the news. Everything's okay in New York, I guess. The Harlem Art Center is slowly shutting down, especially now that the Depression seems to be almost over."

"That was to be expected." I sighed. "But where will the students and teachers go after this?" So that the family wouldn't hear me, I whispered, "But that's not my problem now. What else is new?"

"I heard that Mary Brady and Alain Locke got the Baltimore Museum of Art to put on the first ever museum exhibition of Negro Art."

A jolt ran through me. My voice probably sounded as bitter as a lemon when I responded, "My *Gamin* or *Realization* would have been perfect pieces for that, but Brady doesn't value my work."

"I also heard that a whole room is being dedicated to Jacob Lawrence's forty-one paintings in his *Touissant L'Ouverture* series."

I dropped the phone, then picked it up by its dangling wire. "I have to go," I said and got off the phone so suddenly that Anne probably didn't know what to make of it.

Mr. Jones asked in a concerned voice, "Is there something wrong, Miss Savage?"

"No, well yes, it's a business matter. If you'll excuse me, I'll retire again to my room."

Jacob Lawrence. That little traitor. He used to come to the Artist's Guild meetings. I saved him from working in menial jobs for the rest of his life. He knew my frustration with Brady and the WPA who preferred White supervisors and didn't respect my judgment. He knew how the rest of us in our little group of thinkers felt. And now he goes with Brady.

With semi-strangers in the rest of the house, I couldn't yell. I took my handkerchief and kept twisting it. I started breathing hard.

I lay on my bed and tried to slow down my breathing. In my mind, I went to the darkest of places. But then I got an enlightenment. Perhaps I was taking this too personally. Jacob was probably so happy to have the opportunity to exhibit his work in a real museum that he never considered how it might hurt my feelings. And he might not have known that the Harmon Foundation rejected my work so rudely. I didn't exactly advertise that.

When that realization came to me, a worse thought took root in me: *my work just isn't that good.* Although Jacob's work was getting the most praise, the critics were also lauding a couple other former students of mine. *My work just isn't that good* kept running through my mind. I cried into my pillow as quietly as possible for at least a half hour.

But then I had another thought, Jacob's work sells partly because it's very abstract and uses entrancing colors that almost get your mind away from the atrocities he sometimes captures. The student who recently sold the decorative painting was able to sell it, because it was decorative. My works are all realistic, sometimes gut-wrenchingly so. I sculpted them almost perfectly, but White people don't want to spend money to see Negroes in that kind of way.

I felt like some cruel surgeon was tying my stomach in knots.

Finally, I decided I didn't want to run after success anymore. That door at the top of the stairs never opened widely enough to let me enter the room.

The plan was for me to visit other cities and then return to Chicago. However, if I completed the tour and returned to Chicago, I might climb to the top of one of the city's new skyscrapers and jump.

The next morning I told my host family that due to an emergency I had to get back to New York City. I re-wrapped *Gamin,* the *Dahomean Woman*, Johnson's bust, and the small sculptures. I tried to place them in a large foldable grocery cart I had brought along. After my presentation, I had hoped the cart would be empty, but it was overflowing. Since I couldn't fit everything, I put two of my very small whimsical works under the bed. At least one Negro family would have art by a Negro artist...whether they wanted it or not, whether they found it or not.

I used the family's phone to call the Architectural League and asked them to ship

Realization back to the WPA room. The man on the phone said, "We were hoping you could sell it. I don't think there's any money left in the budget to ship it back."

"Fine, fine," I said quietly but ferociously, "Just let it rot in Chicago."

Outside, it was cold but clear as I boarded the train in downtown Chicago. All the way back to New York I fretted about what I would do with my life. I had achieved some fame, and I loved to sculpt, but I couldn't live on art that was not purchased.

When I arrived at Penn Station in New York City and walked into the night air, I was slapped in the face with icy, blowing snow. Having a few dollars left, I hailed a cab.

The cabbie said, "Quite a night, isn't it? The way the wind's blowing the snow sideways makes it tough to see."

I was quiet, thinking of how hard it would be to lug my shopping cart and suitcase up the slippery steps of my building. When we arrived, the friendly driver was kind enough to assist me up the stairs to the outside door.

"You're a little woman to be handling all this stuff," he said.

Always independent, I said, "I can do it, but thanks for your help." I opened my purse to give him an extra tip, but he wouldn't take it.

After I entered the foyer and unlocked the door, I jumped back. I was sure one of those government men was peeking around the first landing.

I yelled, with all my might, "Get back!"

Although it felt like my paranoia again, I was certain that someone was there.

However, all was quiet. So, I mustered my courage and dragged my stuff up the first flight of stairs.

Then I thought for sure I saw Joe Gould looking around the banister of the second flight. "Get away, Joe!" I screamed. At that moment, an unfamiliar woman came down the stairs. She passed by as quickly as she could.

I stayed put for a while. I felt sure I heard furtive footsteps up on the third landing. But after the woman acted afraid of me, I didn't want to make a scene. So, I quietly and bravely dragged my stuff up the stairs, my teeth chattering with fear the whole time. Thankfully, I made it to my apartment without being attacked. I breathed a sigh of relief.

As I entered, I said to myself, *Now you can finally rest.* I locked the door, secured the chain and put down my suitcase and cart. I unwrapped my sculpture pieces, and again placed my biggest ones on the long, narrow table in the living room.

Meanwhile, the wind shook my front and back windows. I tried to ignore the noise, put on my nightgown and dove into bed.

Just let me sleep, I prayed. But the wind and shaking windows seemed to have a voice. I could swear they were howling at me, "Failure! Failure!" I put my pillow over my head, but that didn't help.

I got up, dashed past my sculptures and went to my kitchen pantry shelf where I remembered I had an old bottle of bourbon. I brought it to bed with me and drank half of it quickly, straight from the bottle.

The next morning in my hung-over state, I called Irene. She was staying with a new boyfriend, a nice older gentleman, and his little girl. When I talked with her, I tried to act nonchalant. "Hi, how ya doin'?"

She filled me in on her latest news, and when she asked about my Chicago trip, I got quiet. "Is there something wrong?" she asked.

"No, nothing." I tried to sound cheerful.

"You're back early. Sounds like it didn't go as well as you expected." The phone went quiet for a while. "I'm sorry, Mom." She paused again, maybe trying to figure out what more to say. "What do you think you'll do now?"

The question struck terror in my heart. As usual, I became combative when Irene said something I didn't like. "Must you pressure me, Irene?"

Irene sighed. We talked about little things, and then hung up. Poor Irene. She had meant well, but I had berated her again.

Every ounce of my confidence and determination slipped away. I couldn't face my fellow artists in New York City anymore. Oh, I could make my trip sound like everything had gone well. However, what I remembered most was hearing about Jacob Lawrence's show with the Harmon Foundation and knowing that no one wanted to buy my work. I couldn't relive all that.

I took to my bed and my "nothing state." Except for an occasional glass of water or a bite of food, I didn't get up much. Irene was still at her boyfriend's. She had told me his name was Leonard Allen and that he had an adorable four-year-old daughter named Lorraine. Before I'd left for Chicago Irene had told me—all excited—that Leonard had proposed and she had said *yes*. I was happy for her.

Two days later I got moving a little and decided to turn on Irene's radio. Static ruined the beautiful notes of a Schubert waltz. So, I called my daughter and used my nicest voice (still feeling guilty about hollerin' at her) to ask what to do about the radio.

"Why don't you go to that place down the street? I think it's called 'Willie's Repair.'"

"I don't think I can, Irene. I'm so tired." Little did she know how tired I was...tired of living.

"I'll tell you what, Mom. They make house calls. I'll phone them and have em' send someone over."

237

"That would be great," and then I said the words I never thought would tumble out of my mouth. "Love ya."

To my utter delight, the guy they sent over was David—the subject of my *Gamin* bust. I had not seen him for so long. We talked and talked, and I was happy that this young man had found his niche in life—repairing things. He was in his early twenties now and rented a room down the street from me. Gradually, I confided in David that I wanted to get away for a while but couldn't afford a fancy vacation. He told me he would check with his uncle in a town called Saugerties, New York, up by the Catskill Mountains. David had heard that his uncle was looking for people to rent his deceased parents' dilapidated house. He kept it for sentimental reasons.

He added, "It might be an interestin' place to get away to for a little while, though you might miss New York City too much."

Little did David know how much I wouldn't miss New York City.

On my fourth day after returning from Chicago, I called James Weldon Johnson's wife and asked her to pick up his bust. The library wanted it back some day but said she could keep it for a year, since the real James had been taken from her so tragically. When Mrs. Johnson arrived, she asked how my exhibition had gone. I said, "Fine, fine," but then she looked at me very intently and asked that haunting question, "What are you going to do now?"

That question was the same question Irene had just asked me. I quickly gave Mrs. Johnson the bust, smiled at her as sweetly as I could, and said I had to cut short my visit because I suddenly felt ill.

When I heard that question again, "What are you going to do now?," I had immediately thought, *My future is hopeless*! My ears started ringing and when she left I yelled, "Why didn't I get asked to exhibit my work? Why didn't anyone in Chicago buy

238

my work?" That's when I destroyed two of my sculptures. That's when I began my lengthy life review.

Part Five

THIRTY-FIVE

The act of recollecting so much over the last few days put me into a dream-like state. I had to say to myself, *Gussie, Gussie, wake up and make some sense out of your memories. You could get lost in thinking about everything, but you've got to move forward. Use your recollections to figure out why you have those savage heart attacks and what to do next.*

I took a deep breath and went to the kitchen. I got a glass of water and returned to my couch to draw some conclusions. After a few minutes, I decided to write them down. I even numbered them.

1.) Going back to the beginning, Daddy may have set a bad example by the way he used the switch when I wouldn't listen. Maybe that's partly why I had a hot temper and I set James' food flying when he wouldn't listen to me. Yet Daddy's standing up for his convictions was a trait I'm glad I copied when I stood up for racial equality with Fontainebleau and the WPA hiring practices.

2.) My mama's predicting my certain success led me to dreaming with more daring than most other Colored children in the Deep South. This made me work extra hard to succeed with my sculpting, but it made me feel like a failure when I couldn't sell my work.

3.) The heavy hand of racism blocked many of my hopes and dreams. That caused some of my savage heart attacks starting with Fontainebleau and going all the way to people not buying my art, because I sculpted Negroes.

4.) Then there were the losses. When John and Robert were taken from me suddenly in the prime of their lives, I was so devastated that I didn't have the energy to go into a savage state. Instead, I went into my "nothing state." But when Roberta was taken from me, I rose up and exploded. If my family hadn't restrained me, I may have torn apart the whole house.

5.) Being robbed of my job at the Harlem Community Arts Center was almost as painful as losing a loved one. The way it happened made me come close to destroying someone and not just something.

6.) In New York City, mean people were a factor. Joe Gould stalking me, J. Edgar Hoover spying on me, Mary Brady robbing me of a chance to exhibit, and Gwendolyn Bennett taking my job. Those people made me angry, suspicious, and paranoid. It was odd to me that I hadn't had any savage heart attacks when Joe made me so mad. I guess I felt he wasn't worth the energy.

7.) It might have helped if I wasn't so independent. Looking back, I wish I had cultivated some deep friendships. The people in my poetry group were friends, but they weren't people I went to with my deepest, innermost feelings. Anne Bennis was my closest friend, but even with her I could be distant and moody. My extreme self-reliance helped me concentrate on my sculpting but led to me bottling up too much.

8.) I counted seven-maybe eight-savage heart attacks over the course of my life. The problem was that they were becoming more severe. When I clumped all the attacks together they had four common threads. Something devastating and shocking happened. It was extremely unfair and unjust. I felt completely powerless. The event was so *overwhelming that my mind quit working and my body took over.*

As I mulled over these things, *Gamin* looked at me with his pensive, wise eyes. He seemed to say, "You've had a wonderful but very rough life, kind of like mine. Forgive yourself for getting mad at times."

Then my *Dahomean Woman* piped up. Even though she was still as a stone, her pose inspired me. She seemed to say, "Take a lesson from me. Look up and out to the future. Your poor heart has been broken so many times it's a miracle that it's still beating. Find a path that brings you peace."

I felt the weight of the world fall from my shoulders. Now the art I created to speak to others was speaking to me.

Finally, everything made sense. I understood why, in certain very crushing situations, I lost my temper in such a destructive way.

Now I had to answer the question that made me act like a crazy person: *What will I do next?*

Continue to sculpt? I'd have more savage heart attacks, because—aside from occasional commissions—people would not buy the kind of work I felt called to create.

Commit suicide? I was afraid God would never forgive me.

Commit homicide? I would certainly not be forgiven if I killed my enemies.

Work in a laundry to make ends meet? Way too humiliating.

Escape mysteriously when everyone thought I was at the height of my career? Now that carried a certain appeal.

I called Irene. She was still at Leonard's. I was happy for her. At the age of thirty-three, she wasn't getting any younger. I must have sounded odd, because Irene asked, "What's gotten into you now, Mom?"

"Come home for a little while and I'll explain. Okay?"

When she opened the door, she saw me in my dirty dress. Little shards of clay remained on the floor. I'm sure Irene knew something was up.

She stared at the slender table that held just four instead of its usual six sculptures. I told her how I had snapped, but I tried to reassure my daughter who had gone through so much with me. "I know it looks bad, but I don't want you to worry. I won't be having these explosions any more."

Irene just stared at me, as though she was afraid I'd end my life to end my troubles. She knew very little about my explosions, because I usually had them when I was alone.

"I've figured it all out now…"

"What are you talking about, Mom?" she asked impatiently.

"It doesn't matter, Irene. I've figured out what to do."

"Oh, and what would that be?"

"I will leave New York City. I have a destination in mind." And then I told her about the house in Saugerties.

Irene groaned. After giving me a million reasons as to why I shouldn't go, she finally said, "Let's just look at it first before you decide."

She called her Leonard. He agreed to take us in his boss' car. Three days later, we took off. Irene sat in the front, and I sat in back with little Lorraine.

As we got further and further away from the city, I took in the beauties of the open land, green trees, and rolling hills. After about two hours, a sign announced that we had arrived in Saugerties. When we pulled off the main road, I could see that the town was as small as an anthill in comparison to NYC, but it did have a post office, a couple of restaurants, several churches and a general store. The only thing I didn't see was another Negro, and that was a concern.

I told Irene and Leonard that the house owned by David's uncle was on a road called Niger Road.

When she saw a second g was missing, Irene bellowed, "This was once Nigger Road. Do you really want to live in a town with a road named like that?"

I was scared. My right hand trembled, but I couldn't let Irene know. "Maybe the people have changed."

Irene turned around and gave me the evil eye. "Are you the same woman who once stood up so fervently for our race?"

"Well, maybe I've changed," I said quietly.

Despite its terrible name, the road was beautiful, narrow, and tree-lined. It crossed a creek and ended at a house at the edge of a steep hill. Just like David predicted, it was dilapidated. However, it was a house. I hadn't lived in a house since my days at West Palm Beach. In front of it was a gigantic piece of grass-covered, cleared land that slanted downward.

Irene and I got out. To the west of the house was a chicken coop. The cackling of the chickens brought me back to my youth in Green Cove Springs. Close by was another coop. I heard lots of cooing and flapping of wings, and when I approached it, I saw pigeons. There was also a shed. When I spotted an outhouse, Irene must have noticed it at the same time, because she said in a voice full of outrage, "An outhouse? We've had indoor plumbing and a toilet in New York City for years."

Irene's fiancé and his daughter said they'd wait in the car. Irene and I went up on the house's little porch and pushed open the unlocked door. Towards the left was a kitchen area.

Irene scowled. "Oh, Mother, a wood-burning stove, and a sink with…what is this?"

"It's a pump, Irene."

Irene touched the pump with obvious disdain. "You mean when you want water you have to pump it?"

244

"Looks like it." Changing the subject as fast as I could, I said, "Let's go upstairs."

"Wait. Before we go, where are the light switches?"

This was getting embarrassing, especially with Irene's accusatory tone. My pride faltered, and I couldn't muster the confidence to put my daughter in her place. "Look," I said brightly, "There's a kerosene lamp on this table."

I should have known this would not pacify Irene. She let go of one of her loudest derogatory grunts in history. "Ugh! No electricity even! What are you going to do without a refrigerator and...and...a radio?"

I wondered myself but quickly said, "Let's go upstairs."

The second floor was like an attic, but you could stand up in it. The room was full of cobwebs and dust that made us both cough. Of course, Irene had to wave her hand dramatically in front of her mouth as if trying to bat away the bad air. However, I noticed that the windows and the roof had nice angles that let in lots of sunlight. I thought, *Maybe I can make this space into a cozy bedroom.*

When we went back downstairs, I looked Irene in the eyes and said almost apologetically, "I have to try this."

"You're crazy. If I could, I would literally drag you out of here and force you back to a civilized place like New York City." Looking around and shaking her head, Irene continued, "How will you take care of yourself with no electricity and no running water? How will you support yourself? I don't make enough at the laundry to help you much."

I hid my anxiety and tried to sound cheerful. "Everything will be all right."

Before she left, Irene insisted she and Leonard take me into town to get food and supplies.

She scowled, "Guess we can't get you anything that needs to be refrigerated."

When we returned, Leonard and little Lorraine carried in the groceries.

Irene and I brought in a few of my belongings—my *Gamin* sculpture, a suitcase, a book of poems by James Weldon Johnson and a pistol I hid in a laundry bag. I'd be prepared if Joe Gould or some G-man showed up.

Shaking her head, Irene said, "Well, good luck. I imagine this place doesn't even have a phone. See if you can walk into town and use a phone booth …or write."

As mean as she sounded, Irene's face was fractured with the same doubt and fear I tried to hide.

"Thank you so much, you and Leonard, for getting me settled in." I knelt down and put my hand on little Lorraine's head. "And, Lorraine, it was really nice sitting with you on our way out here. Come again and visit me."

Lorraine smiled like she'd really enjoyed my company.

"Oh, and, Irene, please don't tell anyone where I went. I don't want my old friends knowing. They wouldn't understand. Especially don't tell Joe Gould or any strangers that might show up at your door."

"Strangers?" Irene asked, like I'd lost my mind.

"Like G-men."

Irene looked like she was a lot more worried about me than any G-men.

We exchanged tentative hugs, not knowing how this would all turn out. She refrained from saying it (thank God), but I knew what Irene was thinking: *I never thought my semi-famous mother would end up like this.*

When they left, the sun had almost disappeared behind the mountains. I went to turn on the kerosene lamp but found there was no kerosene. Luckily, we had purchased candles. I lit them, but I didn't know what to do with myself. I hadn't read by candlelight since my childhood in Green Cove Springs. It was as quiet as a dead man's tomb. But then I heard the *whoooing* of a faraway owl, and it comforted me.

The quiet reminded me that I was definitely not in New York City anymore, just like the sounds of the city had once reminded me as a young woman that I was not in Florida anymore. When Nature called, I walked with a candle's uncertain guidance to the outhouse. My ankles turned slightly as I stepped into unanticipated holes. The outhouse was full of spider webs and flies. When I made it back to the house and collapsed on my dusty bed, I asked myself, *What have I gotten myself into?*

Thankfully, after a couple of weeks I began to settle in. Minus a lot of noisy little sisters and brothers, Saugerties reminded me of living in Green Cove Springs. I enjoyed waking up to the chirping of birds and looking at the landscape outside, knowing that the Hudson River was close by just like the St. John's River was close to my childhood home. However, sometimes my hand trembled again, and I was as surrounded by self-doubt as much as by the Catskill Mountains.

The owner of the house came by. He asked me if my visit would be short term or if I wanted to stay longer. I told him I wanted to stay on indefinitely—as long as possible.

It was fine by him if I wanted to stay forever. He explained that I'd only have to pay $10 a month for rent if I gave him the chickens' eggs and the profits from strangling the pigeons when they were four months old. *Strangling pigeons? What's wrong with this man?* The pigeon part sounded bizarre until he explained he had been selling them to specific, high-class restaurants in New York City that served squabs (baby pigeons). He said this would be my job, if I was willing to accept the deal, and I'd have to give him the profits. It sounded daunting, but I'd been a farm girl and thought I could handle it.

I started a big garden like my parents.' I went into town and, after a while, got introduced to a man named Herman Knaust who hired me to keep records at his fancy cancer research laboratory. Mr. Knaust ended up being my lifesaver. I was not surprised to find that his family had a long history of helping others get on their feet. I sprinkled my alone times with socializing (my reminiscences taught me that I needed people more than I had previously thought). I recited by heart Shakespeare's sonnets to Mr. Knaust's mother's group of lady friends. I got to know and enjoy the children who found their way to my place, and I cooked them chicken foot soup. But I still didn't get really close to anyone...the kind of close where you tell someone your deepest, darkest secrets.

Mr. Knaust bought me clay, and I made a couple of busts of the kids for their parents as well as a commissioned bust of Poultney Bigelow, a local historian. Mr. Knaust also got my house painted and gave me a beat-up, old car. He told me this was the least he could do for such a fine employee, but I knew he had a good heart and wanted to share his blessings with others. I taught the neighbor children a little about sculpting. We played Chinese checkers. I went to church. I strangled the young pigeons and brought them to NYC.

I enjoyed my gardening and actually didn't mind living like a farmer back in the 1800s. Most importantly, I didn't have any savage heart attacks.

However, something gnawed at my heart, something that kept me from being fully content. I didn't know what it was.

Irene wrote to tell me that my friends and acquaintances couldn't believe I left. She kept the location of my hideout a secret, but she also said people kept saying, "Your mom was at the height of her career and only in her forties. How could she leave everything behind?'

Actually, I was more like fifty when I left, but I was glad that I disappeared before the world knew how bad my art career had become. I had my pride.

The jig was up for me when on a snowy evening I went to deliver pigeons to a fancy New York City restaurant. As I pulled into the alley, I looked out my window and came face-to-face with someone on the sidewalk. My heart sank when I saw it was Countee Cullen. When he laid eyes on me, I knew I couldn't hide anymore. My dead pigeons were in wooden boxes in the back seat, because my trunk wouldn't open. I hoped Countee wouldn't notice the stray feathers sticking out.

Countee and I ended up having a nice conversation. He made me so comfortable that I disclosed my move to Saugerties. I surprised myself by mentioning he could bring the old gang out to my place. When he seemed interested, I knew I would have to abandon my pride and let my friends in on my humble existence.

A month later most of the members of our former poetry group—including Anne Bennis—came. It was so nice to see them again. After a few laughs over my hermit lifestyle in a broken down house, we danced and talked until dawn. They accepted everything about my choice—except for the outhouse. I warned them not to tell Joe Gould where I was. Countee told me he heard Joe Gould was in another mental hospital—one that did electric shocks and lobotomies. Actually, I felt somewhat sorry for the man, but, after twenty years or so of fearing Joe Gould's stalking, I was glad to be far away from him.

In the back of my mind, I'd been thinking of this period in Saugerties as one of gradual decline in a pretty environment away from the pressures of the

New York art world. But that got boring. So, I tried to look at my life in a more uplifting way. I thought back to a Bible verse that Daddy often quoted in his own way, "For everything there is a season: a time to be rich, a time to be poor..." One day I walked outside when the trees were turning orange and gold. The leaves rustled under my feet. The sky was a bright blue with white, puffy clouds. My chickens and pigeons were chirping with pleasure. I thought of James Weldon Johnson's song, "Lift Every Voice And Sing," and I belted out each word. I thought I should appreciate this season

Yet something still didn't sit right with me. I'd be going along all cheerful-like, but then in the midst of doing some simple job like pulling weeds or sweeping the steps, I'd feel something like sadness, anger or guilt or a mixture of all of them. I didn't know what it was.

And then I had a dream. In a dark hallway, I walked up a steep staircase. Each step was far above the other. It was a difficult climb. However, I finally made it to the top where there was a little landing and a big door. The door had a lock on it. I had a few keys and tried them, but none opened the lock. I shook the door handle with all my might, but it wouldn't budge. The dream was much like the fantasies and dreams I'd had in my past. Its significance was pretty obvious. No matter how much I wanted to be satisfied with this period of my life, the door to the room containing success never opened. And this still troubled me.

THIRTY-SIX

When I was about fifty-six, something totally unexpected changed my world. I heard a roaring outside. I looked through the window to see a vehicle kicking up dust on my seldom-used road. Much to my amazement, I saw a long, black limousine with two sets of headlights, lots of chrome, and a glittering hood ornament.

A chauffer got out, went to the back door, and opened it. A Negro woman wearing a boa, lots of make up and a dress with a plunging neckline alighted. She had gained a few wrinkles since I'd seen her in Paris, but I immediately knew who she was: Josephine Baker. My premonition came true.

Looking dismayed about the footing, Josephine frowned and almost tripped in her high heels. I glanced at my small wall mirror and tried to pat down my frizzy gray-black hair. I dressed up when I went into town, but on this day I had on one of my regular old white muslin dresses.

Josephine knocked a couple times. I stood by the door, took a deep breath, and opened it. At first, I just stared. It was unreal that Josephine Baker had come all this way to see me.

I smoothed my dress, wishing I wasn't so out of step with my visitor's elegance.

I cried, "Josephine! What a nice surprise! Come in."

She entered and gave me a little hug.

"It's so nice to see you. You're as glamorous as ever!" I said with all the enthusiasm I could muster for this unexpected visit.

Then I had to ask "What in heaven's name made you come all this way to the middle of nowhere?"

"I was performing in New York City and had some free time. I have money, Gussie, and it was no big deal to pay my chauffer to bring me out here," she said nonchalantly.

"Thanks for thinking of me." I was still mystified though.

She looked around, then forced a smile. "I wanted to know where you were and what you were doing. I got in touch with Countee Cullen and asked him, 'Whatever happened to Gussie Savage?' He gave me your address and directions. He said he and your old poetry group had visited and enjoyed their stay, but that, no offense, you live like an old-time farmer."

I managed a nervous laugh and said, "It's not such a bad life, but have a seat, Josephine, although I don't know if you'll want to sit on my old couch. Maybe I could bring out a kitchen chair inst…"

Josephine shrugged. "Don't worry."

She sat down and gazed around the room, looking like she wondered if she made the right decision coming here. Then she flashed one of her brilliant smiles. "Even though I only talked with you a couple times in Paris you made a big impression on me."

My right hand quivered. Darn that nervous habit since I moved to Saugerties. "You definitely made a big impression on me. Can I get you some tea?"

"No, thanks." She paused for a moment before she asked, "Remember our talk at the cafè in Paris? Back then, we were both doing big things, but I said we should check in the newspapers and radio to see what we'd do later with our lives."

"I do remember." I was afraid I turned out to be a big disappointment. "But I was just an art student back then and you were a famous entertainer."

Josephine continued, "I was sure we'd both do even greater things. Across the ocean, I saw that photo of you on the front of *Life* when you were

252

helpin' kids through the WPA. Then I saw a picture of your sculpture for The World's Fair. I wish I coulda actually seen that big harp with all our Negro children, but I wasn't in town then. You accomplished a lot, Girl, just like I thought you would!"

I frowned. "I don't know about that, but I've seen your picture in the paper a couple times too, bringing in large crowds for your shows."

She laughed. "That's not the half of it. I've been doin' a lot of other stuff that people don't know about. But, before I tell you, show me 'round your place."

"You can see it's not fancy, but I like it." I rose and gestured for her to follow. "Like in the kitchen here you can see my stove and sink..."

Standing there in the kitchen area, Josephine looked at me with concern. "Gussie, I'm sure you can tell I'm a woman who speaks her mind. Why do ya have a pump in your kitchen sink? Don't you have plumbin'?"

"No, I don't, and I don't need it," I said, assuredly.

"And you're usin' an old wood-burnin' stove, I see."

"Yep," I said in a voice that was not proud, but not ashamed either.

She walked over to where my lamp sat on a table. "Another thing. I don't want to be rude, but I hope this kerosene lamp is for decoration and you really have electricity."

At that moment I was glad that Mr. Knaust had recently put in electricity for me. "I have electricity."

"Good, but you're somethin' else, Gussie." Josephine shook her head and chuckled.

"Let me show you the upstairs," I said. And so, I brought Josephine to the second floor—the room that gave me calluses from working so hard to fix up. It was my bedroom. I had a pretty quilt on the bed and some pictures on the wall. Josephine said, "Nice," but I could tell she still was not impressed.

We went downstairs and sat down on the couch again. Not one to shilly-shally around, she finally got to the point. "Why did you move way out here when you were accomplishin' so much in New York City?"

"Do you have a few days?"

She laughed.

"I'm serious."

She sat quietly, digesting my offer. "How about if you give me the short version? First, I'll go outside and tell my chauffer I'll double his tip if he waits. By the way, do you have a bathroom?" When I hesitated, she said, "Let me guess—you use an outhouse."

"I'm afraid so."

Shaking her head, Josephine said, "I'll go see the chauffer… and the outhouse."

After she came back in, I said, "I'm sorry I only have the outhouse. But, you know what, moving out here was the only solution I could come up with, and I rather like it."

"You remember from our talk in Paris, I've lived in worse circumstances, Gussie. But continue about why you chose this life."

Hesitantly, I tried to explain, "I hate to admit it, but I 'snapped' right before I came here."

"Tell me about it." Josephine took a deep breath that told me she had times of trial too. "Sometimes I feel like I could snap."

I told Josephine about how I became angry after Irene and Mrs. Johnson asked me what I would do next, about how I imagined my sculptures were calling me a "failure" and how I had destroyed two of my most beloved pieces. Feeling tears trickling down my cheeks, I wiped them away as quickly as I could. Josephine took my hand briefly. Then I told her about some other things that led up to my outlandish behavior.

In Paris, I had already told Josephine about my early life. So, I tried to summarize what went on since. Not wanting to cry again, I didn't hit on my worst moments. At times, Josephine interjected with comments about her life.

After about a half hour, I asked, "How about if I pump you some water? You must be thirsty by now." Josephine quipped, "Yeah, pump me some of that probably dreadful well water."

I pumped it. She drank it but made an unhappy face.

I asked Josephine, "Before I tell you more, what great new and different things have you been doing?"

"You'll never believe it, Gussie." She paused to add dramatic effect to her next statement. "I became a spy."

"What? Don't tell me you got a job with J. Edgar Hoover."

"Hell no! All that guy wants is to make us Negroes miserable." After shaking her head vehemently, like she was trying to toss off any thought of Hoover, she continued, "Here's the story. In 1939 when France declared war on Germany for takin' over Poland, the French got me to be a spy. I used my reputation as a fun, party girl to hob nob with German officers. I got information from them by hearin' them talk about their war plans. Then I reported everything back to the French.

After one of my shows, I flirted with a German general. He invited me up to his hotel room, thinkin' we'd have a good time. I told him to take a shower before we played. While he showered, I took papers out of the middle of a pile on the desk, and left. My superiors congratulated me, sayin' those were very important papers."

Sitting up extra straight with mock seriousness, Josephine crowed, "I take full credit for ending World War II. Just kiddin.' Most people don't know that many women worked as spies durin' the war."

"I didn't know that," I said.

"After the war, I received the Croix de guerre and the Rosette de la Résistance. I was made a Chevalier of the Légion d'honneur by General Charles de Gaulle."

Before I could congratulate her, Josephine's chauffeur honked, and she rushed out to give him another tip.

While she went outside, I thought about how it was nice to finally talk with someone, heart-to-heart.

When Josephine returned, she said, "You told me little about your life, but I got a feelin' there's more to your story."

She was right. Pulling at the skirt of my dress like it was a lifeline, I told her more specifically about what troubled me over the years—how my loved ones died so tragically, how I felt compelled to sculpt my Negro brothers and sisters but received little money for it, and how I helped talented young people in Harlem become artists only to have Gwendolyn Bennett take that privilege away from me. I told her how my lifelong dream of climbing that staircase and entering the door to a room containing my success never came true. And I told her in more detail about my savage heart attacks.

Josephine took a long, serious look at me. "I can understand why you came here now. You wanted to get away from all those frustrations. That anger you kept feeling, those explosions, what did you call 'em... 'savage heart attacks?' They had to be scary." She looked at me with the eyes of a loving mother. "You had so many disappointments and losses."

How sweet it was to be understood!

But then Josephine said, "When I hear you talking about climbin' that stairway to success, it makes me think of somethin'. Somethin' I never gave much thought to before. You may not want to answer this. I know it will be hard and I don't want to offend you."

"My goodness, Josephine, spit it out. You don't seem to be one to mince words."

She took a deep breath. "How much do you think pride coulda been tied up with your wantin' to succeed?"

I knew it was hard for Josephine to be so direct about this. She caught me completely off-guard. I didn't know what to say...or think. I stuttered, "Wh...What do you mean? I knew I had a gift. My mother said I was destined for success. I created my art for..." I was confused. I started wondering why I did create my art.

"Like I said, Gussie, I don't want to upset you, but maybe you...and probably me...have let pride get in our way sometimes."

"I don't know if I understand."

"It sounds like you created those little clay animals just because you wanted to without carin' what anyone else thought, but as life went on, maybe you wanted too much to be admired for your accomplishments...which by the way tempts all of us in the public eye."

My hand shook, and I felt my face contort into a scowl. I didn't like what Josephine was saying. "I loved creating every piece of art I ever made. As an adult, I still felt happy whenever I was sculpting— like that little kid at the clay pit."

"But then you had to put up with people's reactions to your art, right?"

"Yep, that was the hard part. When I did the commissioned busts, people always loved them. When I branched out to other forms of sculpture, people with money said they loved them, but then they didn't buy them."

At this point, I stood up and walked over to my desk and got out a picture. It was the frayed photo of my *Realization* sculpture. "You probably never heard about this sculpture of mine."

Josephine studied it. "It's beautiful. And sad. The man and woman look so real I feel they might move at any minute."

"I displayed it at two exhibitions attended by a lot of rich people. No individual, no museum, no nothing bought it."

"That's pathetic!" said Josephine in an angry voice. "I can see why you got mad, even got tempted to give up your art."

"Now you know why I started feeling like a failure," I said, finally feeling understood.

We both sat quietly with our thoughts. Then Josephine asked, "You took the people's not buyin' em to heart, didn't you? And then that question, 'What will you do next?' seemed like a judgment—that you might as well quit doin' what you're doin' now because it ain't workin.'"

"Yeah, that question was the final blow to my confidence," I said with a deep sigh.

Josephine put her hand on mine and said in the sweetest way, "But it wasn't that you were a failure." She paused. "The fact was it wasn't time for your art to be appreciated."

I felt the need to stand up for myself, "What could I do, Josephine? I had to support myself and I had things to say to the world."

"If you coulda just stayed with those two thoughts—you needed to support yourself and you wanted to express yourself. Then you might not have destroyed your sculptures."

I let out a loud sigh. "This is hard for me to digest. It's a whole new way of looking at things."

Josephine smiled in sympathy. "It's a new way of thinkin' for me too. I never gave much thought to this whole success thing. I've just been movin' on, puttin' all my energy into one project after another. But I'm thinkin' back to when I danced with the others in that chorus for *Shuffle Along*. We all had to dance in rhythm with each other. Of course. I loved dancin,' as I told you. When I just concentrated on the steps, I did fine. When I'd start thinkin' about what the audience thought of my dancin,' I'd miss steps."

I gritted my teeth, but I listened to where she was going. Josephine continued, "Any of us who accomplish a lot start needin' people to recognize how good we're doin.' "

I asked in a pouting way, "Should I blame my mama for this? Maybe she should have never predicted I'd be a success someday."

"Naw, I wouldn't blame her. She gave you the confidence to use your God-given talent to sculpt our people so magnificently."

My jaw relaxed a little.

"But she did plant in your head that word "success" and thinkin' about it may have got you in trouble." Like a schoolteacher, Josephine asked, "What's the opposite of success, Gussie?"

"Failure, of course."

"And that's what you thought your sculptures were calling you...a failure."

We both sighed as one. Josephine said, "All this thinkin' is gettin' too hard for me." She looked out the window. "Anyhow, it sure is peaceful here—the birds, the trees, all this land to yourself. I think you made a good choice to come to Saugerties." She paused before she added, "As long as you ain't bitter about that success stuff."

Bitter. To use one of Daddy's expressions, Josephine hit the nail on the head! That was the exact word to describe the vague feeling haunting me since I moved to my little house by the hill.

I thanked Josephine. "You just helped me realize what's bothered me since I moved. I've been bitter."

Changing the subject a little, Josephine said, "This country life calls for more work than I'd like—pumpin' water, the wood stove, the outhouse—but there is a peacefulness to it that I envy."

Running out of patience, the chauffeur began honking his horn. We walked to the front door together. I fussed with a tie on my dress. I knew I would probably never see Josephine again. She stood very close to me. Very gently, she put her hands on each side of my face and tilted my head to look at her.

"Don't you ever forget what I'm gonna tell you, Gussie. You brought our people forward. Your parents had been slaves as children. Look at how you took some of the next generation of Negroes from back-breakin' jobs to becomin' creators of great art. What a jump!"

I smiled, then moved my head out of her tender hold. I wasn't used to this closeness. "Can I get you some eggs from the chicken coop before you go?"

"No, quit changing the subject! What I want from you is to feel that because of your hard work and dedication you did make it into not one but a few rooms. One with your beautiful art showin' our Negro people in all our dignity and sufferin'. One with the thousands of students who you helped. One with all our Colored people who benefited from your stand for equality, and one with thousands of White people who finally got to look at us Black people close-up at the Fair."

Josephine's words made my heart skip a beat...in a good way. I said, "Wow! It's going to take time for all that to sink in, but I appreciate your thoughts."

I walked to the kitchen sink, and pumped a cup of water. "Want one before you go?"

Josephine shook her head no. "Turn and look at me, Gussie. One more thing. Mark my words. Either in your lifetime or after you're gone, people will want your works of art. It may not be the time for a statue like *Realization* now, but someday when people get enlightened, when they care about how much us Negroes suffered, the little that remains of your art will be scooped up by museums and rich people."

"Hard to believe."

Josephine walked over to me and gave me the longest, most loving hug I'd ever had—at least from a woman. Eventually, she pulled back, gave me a quick kiss on the lips, and said, "Time to go."

I held her elbow as she teetered on her heels back to the limo. She rolled down the window. I grabbed her hand one last time.

Her car drove off into the sunset. I stood and watched and waved until she was out of sight.

THIRTY-SEVEN

My mama would have said, "You shouldn't a been surprised that Josephine showed up again. You always gotta listen to your premonitions, Gussie."

After Josephine left, I quit getting that sinking feeling I now realized was bitterness. Every day I thought of what Josephine said. I took it too personally at the end of my career when people didn't buy my work. Any artist would be bothered, but I didn't need to get to the point of such rage.

"What are you going to do next?" I shouldn't have let that question get to me so much. I took it as a criticism, that my work wasn't that good, and I should find something altogether different to do. Maybe Irene and Mrs. Johnson were wondering if I was just going to take a nap or find another venue for exhibiting my art.

I quit using the word "success" in my mind and speech. I realized that the main thing was I contributed a lot to the world. My life had purpose and meaning.

And, besides what I did for "the world," I had led an amazing life: Mingling with some of the top thinkers in Harlem. Studying in Paris. Traveling throughout Europe. Talking to socialites in Chicago. Opening my own gallery. No one in the 1890s would have believed that such things could be possible for a Colored girl growing up in Green Cove Springs.

I didn't have that staircase dream again, and my hand quit quivering. I was finally content with my life in Saugerties.

I had many of what I called "magic moments" like I did when I was at peace on those rare afternoons in my apartment. They happened when, without a care in the world, I sat on my porch rocker or on the hillside behind my house and admired the beauties of nature.

Occasionally I received a letter. I had to go to the post office in town to pick up my mail and only did so a couple times a week. One day I got a letter from Irene. It contained a short article from *Time* magazine. Joe Gould died on August 19, 1957 at The Pilgrim State Hospital. This was the place where they did lobotomies and electro-shock treatments. A funeral was held in Greenwich Village. *Time* said Joe had no known relatives but had well-known friends like poet e.e. Cummings and author William Saroyan. However, none of them attended his funeral.

I felt a little sorry for him, but Joe Gould burned all his bridges behind him and had no one there for him at the end. Now, Praise God, he definitely could not make any unwanted appearances in my life.

Josephine sent me letters once in a while. It was hard to get correspondence back to her because she moved so much. She told me she started adopting children from different countries. She called them her Rainbow Tribe. She wanted to prove that everyone can get along regardless of race or nationality.

In October of 1958, Josephine sent me a newspaper article. It talked about the death of a Negro writer with whom I wasn't familiar, and it went on to talk about how he was a figure from the "The Harlem Renaissance." That was the first time I'd ever heard that phrase. The article said, "'The Harlem Renaissance' lasted from the 1910s through the 1930s. The period was the golden age in Negro culture in Harlem. Through their artistic, literary, and musical achievements, Augusta Savage, Langston Hughes, and other gifted Negroes in Harlem brought respect to their race in the gap between Reconstruction and the Civil Rights Movement." In the margin, Josephine wrote in red pen, "You have now claimed your place in history."

From my spot on the couch, I turned to Gamin and said, "Well, well, I guess it was all worthwhile."

Part Six

THIRTY-EIGHT

With all of my savage heart attacks, I thought for sure a real heart attack would be what would kill me. But, in 1960 at the age of 68, I began experiencing abdominal pain. I went to the doctor in Saugerties. He took x-rays and said it was cancer. Incurable cancer at that. I didn't want to tell Irene; I figured I had worried her enough over the years. However, when she called me one day and I couldn't stifle a moan, she knew something was wrong. I had to confess. She and Leonard came to pick me up and brought me to their apartment in Brooklyn. I fought to hold back tears when I said goodbye to my home, chickens, pigeons, garden, sculpture shed, Mr. Knaust, the neighbor children, and the hillside behind my house.

One day at Irene's apartment, I sat upright propped by pillows on my bed and talked with my daughter and my step-granddaughter Lorraine. "When I'm gone, people may say, 'she died a hermit who ran away from the art world,' but don't you let them get away with that. I was one of the leaders of The Harlem Renaissance. My friends and I in New York City built a bridge that helped our people grow in dignity between the time of the Jim Crow laws and the Civil Rights…"

I stumbled with my words because of the pain… "the Civil Rights Movement. We showed the world that Negroes are equal to Whites. We can produce art, music, and books just as good as any of theirs."

"Is this supposed to be part of a eulogy, Mom?" Irene asked (for once, not sarcastically).

I shook my head. "I don't need a fancy home-going party, but if you hear people say they don't know why I left New York City, just tell them I enjoyed my last years in Saugerties."

When I groaned in pain again, Irene got me a glass of water and put it to my lips. "Thanks, Irene. Tell them Saugerties took me back to my childhood in Green Cove Springs. Please don't tell them about my savage heart ."

"I still don't understand that part, Mom, but if it's real to you, I won't judge,"

Although Lorraine was a young woman now, she looked at me with childlike, inquiring eyes. "What's a savage heart, Grandma?"

"Not everyone has one, Lorraine. It comes from deep pain." I winced, because of the real pain in my stomach. "It comes from suddenly losing what you dearly love. With me it was my baby sisters and brothers, my two good husbands, my newborn baby…"

"That had to be terrible," Lorraine said as she frowned in sympathy.

I reached for a sip of water. "There were more, Baby …my scholarship, my job, my hopes and dreams. If losses like that come often and unexpectedly, you're in deep pain. If you don't know what to do with that pain, you can lose control…."

My step-granddaughter looked puzzled. She knew about my art and where I lived in Saugerties, but otherwise she didn't know much about my life. We didn't sit around talking about those things.

I explained, "Very few people have savage heart attacks. I am one of the few. It won't happen to you. Your life is already much smoother than mine was at your age."

"You mentioned 'hopes' and 'dreams,' Grandma. From the time I met you, you seemed content in Saugerties."

"I did come to lift my voice and sing there, but..."

"But what, Grandma?" This step-granddaughter of mine sure was interested in me.

"From the time I was a little girl, I loved making things out of clay...at first ducks and chickens, but later our people," I told her.." I hoped and dreamed that others would love my work and buy it. They loved my work," I grimaced again, "but for the most part, they didn't buy it."

"That must have made you sad...and mad," Lorraine said with tears clouding her big brown eyes.

I thought of my conversation with Josephine. "Maybe I let it bother me too much."

My daughter shocked me when she said, "You left your mark on the world, Mom. Aside from your beautiful sculptures, I remember all those young street-boys coming to our place. And you spoke up for our people when you needed to." She paused, unfamiliar with giving me praise.

Now it was time for my eyes to fill with tears. "Thank you, Irene."

Irene patted my shoulder, and Lorraine squeezed my hand. They both told me to get some rest.

As they were leaving the room, I wanted to say something more. "Even if the rich White people didn't buy my work, many Whites as well as Negroes gave me a hand up."

Lorraine smiled, and I said, "If someone extends you a hand up, take it, and appreciate it. Okay, Lorraine?"

"I will Grandma," Lorraine said. Irene blew me a kiss.

"Now get some rest, and we'll see ya later," Irene said.

They did see me later, but the pain became so dire that I could speak in only five to six word sentences the next day. By the end of the week, I was down to one or two words at a time. Irene and Leonard took me to Abraham Jacobi Hospital in the Bronx.

As I lay on my hospital bed with my eyes closed, scenes from my life flashed through my mind. I certainly had my share of troubles, but Fate had had some pretty special things in store for this little girl from Green Cove Springs—things that still astonished me.

EPILOGUE

Augusta Savage died on March 26, 1962, at the age of 70. She was buried at Ferncliff Cemetery and Mausoleum in Hartsdale, New York.

Looking at the art history books containing information on Augusta Savage, I have noticed that many of the pictures of her works say "location unknown." Augusta Savage had no idea that these works would be highly valued today. Personally, I would love to find out where *Realization* and *After The Glory* are.

High school history books give a paragraph or two to The Harlem Renaissance, and some specifically mention Augusta Savage, but most adults know little or nothing about the Harlem Renaissance. While Augusta is still not widely known, she has a small but growing following in the art and academic worlds. Jeffreen Hayes has curated the traveling exhibition: *Augusta Savage: Renaissance Woman* at the Cummer Museum of Art and Gardens in Jacksonville, Florida between October of 2018 and March of 2019. It included 80 works of art by Augusta and some of the students she nurtured. The exhibit will travel to other cities.

Augusta would probably be amazed that a handful of dedicated art historians labor to dig up every fact possible about her life. The following are some of the researchers who have written extensively about Savage:

Theresa Leininger-Miller, Associate Professor of Art History at the University of Cincinnati, *The New Negro Artists in Paris. African American Painters and Sculptors in the City of Light, 1922-1934*. Leininger-Miller's book should be in every college and high school library that has an art history program. Her research on Savage is extensive.

Romare Bearden (who knew Savage) and Harry Henderson, *A History of African-American Artists.* These men interviewed people who worked with Savage and thereby collected a treasure trove of information about how Augusta thought and acted.

Amy Kirschke, chair of the Art History Program at North Carolina University, *Women Artists of the Harlem Renaissance.* Kirschke collected writings about these female artists including one by Leininger-Miller about Augusta Savage.

Jill LePore, Professor of American History at Harvard University, *Joe Gould's Teeth.* LePore began by writing about Joe Gould, but when she found that Gould made Savage such an object of his attention she actively researched much of Savage's life also.

Alan Schroeder, author. *In Her Hands, The Story of Sculptor Augusta Savage,* illustrated by JacMe Berreal, This book is recommended for five through eight-year-olds but can be informative to people of any age.

In 2007 the City of Green Cove Springs, Florida nominated Augusta Savage to the Florida Artist Hall of Fame. She was inducted in the spring of 2008. Today at the location of her birth, there is a Community Center named in her honor.

How joyful Augusta would feel to know that schools, galleries, festivals and gardens would also be named after her:

The Augusta Fells Savage Institute of Visual Arts, a public high school in Baltimore, Maryland

The Augusta Savage Gallery at the University of Massachusetts

The Augusta Savage Sculpture Garden at the Douglas Anderson School of the Arts in Jacksonville

The Augusta Savage Friendship Park in Green Cove Springs

The Augusta Savage Cultural Arts Festival held in Green Cove Springs

Augusta's Saugerties home has made it into the national register. Along with Richard Duncan, Karlyn Elia Knaust, (daughter of Herman Knaust) purchased the house. They have worked diligently to restore and preserve it. On display, they have photos of Augusta and her work as well as a small collection of her pieces.

Augusta's favorite haunt, the 135th St. Library, has fondly honored Augusta Savage and the other leaders of The Harlem Renaissance. Now the library has turned into a research and exhibition center known as The Schomburg Center for Research in Black Culture named after Arturo Schomburg who saved and preserved objects relating to Black History. The Countee Cullen Library for the public is next door. Underneath the Schomburg Research Center are buried the ashes of Langston Hughes.

In 1988, the Schomburg Center held a special evening to recognize Augusta Savage. Romare Bearden attended along with a Who's Who of famous Black artists who were schooled by Augusta Savage. Her step- granddaughter Lorraine Lucas came and donated some of Savage's work to the library at the behest of her deceased mother, Irene, who wanted her mother's work to be on exhibit.

Lorraine also attended the dedication of the new prominent sign in Saugerties named Augusta Savage Road—no longer Nigger or Niger Road. On both occasions, she shared having fun with her step-grandmother in her old age. Sadly, Lorraine has departed from this life also.

AUTHOR'S NOTES

I learned about Augusta Savage through a visit with my daughter to view an exhibit of Jacob Lawrence's work at the Detroit Institute of Art. In the gift shop, I purchased a set of playing cards showing the works of African-American artists on one side and a synopsis of the artists' lives on the other. Seeing Gamin with his sad but spunky expression, I became interested. When I turned the card over and read about Savage's career, I became even more interested.

After I researched Augusta Savage, I thought that for all she did as an artist, mentor, educator and civil rights activist, she deserved more recognition in our twenty-first century. That's when I decided to write a book about her life. My goal was not to write a factual history about Augusta Savage's accomplishments and specific works of art. That has been done wonderfully by a handful of dedicated researchers. Rather, my goal was to appeal to a wider readership by giving Augusta Savage a heart and soul. My impression of her inner life is just that—an impression—although based on extensive study. I traveled to all the locations where she lived and absorbed the atmosphere of her surroundings.

While Augusta Savage probably did not use the words "savage heart attacks," I believe that she probably did have outbursts of rage (understandably so). Harry Henderson and Romare Bearden (who knew Augusta personally) interviewed Anne Bennis who told them the Marian Anderson story. They also spoke with some of her students and fellow artists to come up with this description of Savage's temperament: "While she could cajole, coax, humor and laugh, most artists remember that she could at times be very stern, sharp, and demanding, capable of attacking with rage, especially if she felt she was not taken seriously."

I tried to stick with what we know is historically true about Augusta Savage. She did not keep a diary or record of her life. Almost all the characters in the book were real—with the following exceptions. There was no "David," specifically. There are mixed opinions as to whether Ellis posed for *Gamin* or whether a boy from the streets did. So, I combined the two. David's family in Saugerties is made-up. I have attempted to find out who originally owned the house that Savage rented but have been unable to do so. One source said that the boy whom she sculpted for *Gamin* did have family in Saugerties and that the boy did suggest she go up there.

Regarding Josephine Baker, she was in Paris at the same time as Augusta. One researcher said Augusta viewed and was inspired by Josephine's performance. Others say she may not have met her. Augusta and Josephine's conversations were conjured from my imagination. However, everything that Josephine revealed about herself is derived from known facts—her early life, her activities as a spy, etc. Often, in historical fiction, we writers add characters to provide a sounding board for what the main character is thinking and feeling, and Josephine was one.

I also took the liberty of having Arturo Schomburg come into the gatherings of the Harlem Renaissance leaders about ten years later than he actually did, because it helped with the flow of the story. Otherwise, all I wrote about his background and collection activities is true.

I don't think anyone knows how Augusta's first husband died. I imagined the scenario of his death.

Just about every situation regarding Joe Gould did occur. He made Augusta's life miserable by stalking her. The scenarios with Millen Brand and Grace Nail actually did happen also.

Augusta sculpted all of the sculptures I named. I am uncertain about exactly when *After The Glory* and *Realization* were created, but all of my research points to their being lost works of art. Because so many of the pictures of her works are accompanied by the words "location unknown," some people believe that Augusta may very well have destroyed some of her pieces. Then again, some of the smaller ones may have been purchased and today sit on people's mantels.

The archivist for Green Cove Springs has investigated every detail of Augusta's life and says that public records show James Savage divorced Augusta in the 1940s.

All in all, it was not necessary to embellish Augusta Savage's life with a lot of highly imagined drama or characters. Her life was interesting and exciting enough.

ACKNOWLEDGEMENTS

My deepest thanks to...

Mary Custureri, publisher of Taylor and Seale, for seeing the value of this book and wanting to shed light on the accomplishments of Augusta Savage.

Dr. Lynn Hawkins, who helped me with her incredible knowledge of writing, but also with her kindness and support.

Tamie Holmes, English teacher who shared her educational and experiential insights.

Linda Niedringhaus, Beulah Martinez, Jim Klotz, and Ritu Puppula for reading and critiquing my work.

Julius and Cynthia Holmes, who helped me understand the life and language of people raised in the Jim Crow days.

Teresa Leininger-Miller who spoke to me and did such excellent research on Augusta.

Pat Garlinghouse, proprietor of the exquisite River Park Inn Bed and Breakfast in Green Cove Springs, Florida, who showed me the land on which the Fells family lived, the creek next to where Augusta sculpted, and the spring to which tourists flocked years ago.

Vishi Garig, archivist of Green Cove Springs, who furnished me with abundant factual information from census records, etc.

Greeters at The Augusta Savage Cultural Arts Festival who put me in touch with people who may have known about Augusta.

Eugene Francis, whose newspaper-published presentation to the Clay County Historical Society added information that proved helpful.

Maude Jackson, resident of Middleburg (next to Green Cove Springs), who recounted her memories of going to a segregated, one-room schoolhouse in the Jim Crow days and of her work with Dr. Martin Luther King, Jr. in St. Augustine.

Kris Perkins, who accompanied me to do research in New York City.

Tammi Lawson from the Schomburg Research Center who made it possible for me to review records about Augusta and who told me about her in-person contacts with Augusta's step-granddaughter.

Karlyn Knaust Elia who drove me around Saugerties for a full day—showing me her father's research center where Augusta worked, the preserved buildings on their main street, and the terrain of the Catskill Mountains and the Hudson River—all of which were a part of Augusta's later life.

Richard Duncan who is the co-owner of The Augusta Savage House and who helped explain what daily life was like for Augusta in her home and property.

Mary Voss who ventured with me to West Palm Beach to view several of the identical houses for African-American workers in the early 1900s.

Nick Golubov from The Historical Society of Palm Beach County.